WHAT FUTURE ME TOLD PAST ME

GWANSHEMA LADD, LVN

Fort Worth, Texas

Copyright © 2024 by Gwanshema Ladd

All rights reserved.

No portion of this book may be reproduced without written permission from the publisher or author except as permitted by U.S. copyright law.

This publication is designed to provide accurate and authoritative information regarding the subject matter covered. It is sold with the understanding that neither the author nor the publisher is engaged in rendering legal, investment, accounting, or other professional services. While the publisher and author have used their best efforts in preparing this book, they make no representations or warranties concerning the accuracy or completeness of the contents of this book and specifically disclaim any implied warranties of merchantability or fitness for a particular purpose.

Sales representatives or written sales materials may create or extend no warranty. The advice and strategies contained herein may not be suitable for your situation. You should consult with a professional when appropriate. Neither the publisher nor the author shall be liable for any loss of profit or other commercial damages, including but not limited to special, incidental, consequential, personal, or other damages.

Illustration by: Deepti Rai

ISBN: 979-8-3302-2702-0

Gemlight Publishing LLC

Table of Contents

Dedication	4
Introduction	6
Chapter 1 *Don't See Nothin'*	9
Chapter 1 Worksheet	15
Chapter 2 *Don't Say Nothing'*	18
Chapter 2 Worksheet	26
Chapter 3 *I Don't Understand*	30
Chapter 3 Worksheet	37
Chapter 4 *Don't Know What You Don't Know!*	40
Chapter 4 Worksheet	49
Chapter 5 *Does Truth Exist?*	53
Chapter 5 Worksheet	61
Chapter 6 *Who Told You To?*	63
Chapter 6 Worksheet	71
Chapter 7 *Trust Who?*	73
Chapter 7 Worksheet	80
Chapter 8 *Who Am I?*	84
Chapter 8 Worksheet	94
Chapter 9 *Which Path Do I Take?*	99
Chapter 9 Worksheet	106
Chapter 10 *Relationships and Mistakes*	109
Chapter 10 Worksheet	116
Chapter 11 *Are Parents Good or Bad?*	118
Chapter 11 Worksheet	126
Appendix	129
About the Author	131
Acknowledgements	134

Dedication

This book is written in loving memory of my grandmother, Ollie Vee Ladd A.K.A. "Mother Ladd." She was known and recognized as a strong pillar in the West Las Vegas community and beyond! She helped to found "Full Gospel Deliverance church" in downtown Las Vegas, NV. The year 2021 marked thirty years

Unfortunately, I went there after the COVID-19 pandemic ended, and they were closed. However, two to three other churches were birthed out of that church, and they are still up and running today! Mother Ladd's house on little ol' Jackson Street was recognized as a place where hurting people could always go! As a child, her house was really where I grew up. I saw everything coming to her house, from abused family members, black eyes, neglected strangers, the homeless, hungry, disabled, abandoned, and mentally ill. I would ride with Grandma as she drove around the west side, picking kids up and taking them to church. Everyone knew Mother Ladd!

I dedicate this book to a historical woman, General, and the loss of a historical landmark, a safe place. (My grandmother's house.)

I want the world to know that there are jewels in West Las Vegas! The lack of knowledge, wisdom, and understanding is costing the African American communities a fortune! Please keep your grandparents' properties and preserve the historical landmarks if you can!

I love you, Grandmama. You will not be forgotten, nor your legacy to this world, the community, your family, or the Kingdom of God

Thank you for the spiritual groundwork you laid and the spiritual gifts you passed along, as well as the prayers! Thank you for covering your grandchildren with the anointing oil that ran down our foreheads!! It got us through some things!

Rest in peace, and well done! (1992   ) Note: If you enjoy this book, you will also enjoy the albums that tell a story along with the book!!! They are entitled Who am I, and I Am. You can find them on all major streaming sites! (Spotify, Apple, iTunes, Amazon Music, etc.) Listen to a different track with each chapter!

Listen to the track: Shout Outs (album I Am)

Introduction

This book is for teenagers and adults. It is a compilation of resources and key points that would have helped me develop and process the difficulties and dysfunctions of my life at an earlier stage. It would have increased my potential, skills, confidence, outlook on life, self-identity, and direction. I now share these key points with you!'

In short, this book is what future me would tell past me that would have made my future life so much better!

As a licensed vocational nurse and trained minister in the word of God, I see how the slightest interruption in the foundational building period of a child can last a lifetime! Without proper guidance, knowledge, and understanding, it can lead to long-term chronic dysfunction in behavior, emotions, and even physical reactions.

Most people do not believe in getting therapy or undergoing counseling. If you are African American or Latino, your culture does not believe in therapy or counseling! It is quite the opposite! Most cultures of color believe in keeping things quiet and letting the adults handle everything because you will grow out of it and get past it.

Have you ever heard those before? Have you ever heard of this one? What goes on in this house stays in this house!

I wrote this book for those who do not believe in counseling, have not received therapy, and don't even believe in therapy. As you read the following chapters, have a notepad and pencil, a box of tissues, and something to drink.

I pray that you find answers within each chapter and discover healing as you turn each page! Lies will be broken, truths will be revealed, and the love of God will rain over you as you begin to see, feel, and know Jesus in a new way!

This book is for those Christians seeking God or who are not Christian but want to know where God was/is in your situation and what the truth is! Through this book, you should be able to see where God was in every incident, disappointment, and in your life right now, even when you think he was not.

What Future Me Told Past Me is for boys and girls, and men and women! If you have kids already use this book as a guide through parenthood! It offers good tips on how to begin to shape your child's mind, spirit, and emotions in a healthy and balanced way. The results will lead to a successful, well-balanced life and new confidence in your child and parenting!

People have asked me over the years: "Shema, how did you get your kids to be like that?" Well, you will get some of the answers by reading this book!

What is one thing we say once we get tired of our parents? When I have kids, I will never………! (fill in the blank) Well, that's what I held to in principle! I gave my kids everything I believed I should have had to test my theory. Lol! It worked!!!!!!!!!

Now, I choose to share it with others who have identity issues or are still having mommy/daddy issues. No matter your age!! I have the privilege of hearing my kids say, "Mom, my friends ask me why I don't have all the issues they have." Adults ask how I got so much wisdom…. (proof that it works)

Purchase the albums that go along with this book! It's all about Identity!

The first album, Who Am I, is secular, but it will help you find where you are mentally and spiritually and walk over the bridge to Christ! The second album, I Am, is spiritual and will help you draw closer to God!

I pray that the God of Jesus, Abraham, Isaac, and Jacob reveals himself to you today. (John 3:16) May your life never be the same after reading this book! I pray that every person reading this book who is feeling alone, unqualified, insufficient, ugly, shameful, doubtful, confused, lost, less than, unloved, unseen, embarrassed, depressed, or suicidal has the truth revealed to them through this book today. (Psalm 31:1)

I pray that every weapon formed against them shall not prosper (Isaiah 54:17) and that the yolks of bondage, oppression, suppression, and depression be broken off right now in the name of Jesus. I declare freedom for them! I pray that no satanic attack be allowed to hinder your breakthrough (2 Cor. 3:17)

Father, open their eyes and hearts so they can see your plan for their life! Let them hunger and thirst for righteousness, truth, and life in Christ! (John 14:6) Sealed in the blood of Jesus. Amen!

NOTE: At the end of each chapter, there are worksheets to help you identify the hurts and hurdles you must overcome to ensure a successful future! These worksheets will also have daily tools to start healing and becoming a new person, a whole person free from the heavy baggage of the past!

Now, let's get to it!

-Shema

Chapter 1
Don't See Nothin'

Sometimes, I wonder how blind people can see; then, I wonder how people who can see act blind. Maybe it's not an eyesight problem, but something else. I can remember moments of my life from the time I was born. I was always trying to see who I could trust, what was good or bad, or what got positive or negative responses. What is love?

I'm a seventies baby, born and raised in fabulous Las Vegas, Nevada! (Fabulously hot and dry); I grew up in a household they called "domestic violence." In the seventies, pimpin' and hoeing was big! Woodstock was in play with big promotions on smoking marijuana, and the fight for freedom was the theme of the scene! Cocaine, heroin, and crack were dominating our North American culture, and I was born right in the middle of it!

I am the firstborn in my family. I have one younger sister who is five years younger than me; she is an eighties baby. Then, another younger sister is a baby in her nineties. I'm the one old enough to remember the Mafia and mob bosses fighting and killing each other over who was going to run Las Vegas and the hotel Casino industry!

While I watched mafia leaders such as Bugsy Siegel, Lucky Luciano, Al Capone, and the Don going to prison or dying on the news (cars blowing' up, shootings, explosions, people disappearing….), I had a warfare to watch LIVE in my own home! However, we never discussed the violence seen on the news. As I sat and watched TV, I couldn't help but wonder if my parents were going to disappear as the people on the news were. Was I going to die one day because Daddy made a bad deal?

These thoughts crossed my mind frequently since I could feel that my parents were into things I was too young to understand. Unbelievable, right? You may think I'm crazy for thinking that way. What's even crazier is that 2022 the news coverage read: "Lake Meade water level at record low! Barrels found at the bottom of Lake Meade with bodies in them!" Now I know where those bodies disappeared! I'm glad my family wasn't in one of them!

I am now forty-eight years old (2023) and watching Channel 8 news Las Vegas. A woman my age is telling her story about how her dad disappeared when she was a little girl. He never came home. Her dad was one of the bodies found in those barrels! Wow! I'm not crazy, after all.

I see black eyes AND bloody noses. I hear sounds of arguing, begging, vomiting, cracked ribs, adults talking, and silence. I'm not sure what my younger sister sees or hears. However, I have a friend that I have gotten to know quite well. Her name is Neglect. Neglect is not always seen but always felt. I met her when I was old enough to realize mentally what hunger meant.

While I was sitting in my room thinking of food and fun, a huge fist would meet my mother's face while ugly words were being hurled. Any food Mama cooked, Dad would say, "I'm not eating this shit!" He would look at the food and sometimes throw it across the room. No groceries Mama bought was never enough, or by my father's words, "You can't even buy groceries, right?"!

I can see the fear and nervousness in Mother's face and body language as we grocery shopped. She was afraid to bring the food home, and I was nervous. As I watched the food run down the wall and slide onto the floor, I wondered why he was so mad about the food. What does "taste bad" mean? I was so young that I didn't know the difference between tasting bad and tasting good; all I knew was that it was food! The more I saw how Mom was treated, the more I realized I didn't want to be a girl. Boys have it much easier.

My parents were normally not present. Mama was at work, and Daddy was at work as well. If they weren't working, they were partying, Mom was at night school, or Dad was in the garage working on a project of some sort. In the meantime, my sister and I were getting more acquainted. Does anyone see me? See us? I loved to watch Mr. and Mrs.

Huxtable talk to their kids on the Cosby show! That show gave me an example of what I believed was how a family was supposed to be. I know it probably sounds silly, but I didn't have anything else that was nurturing to compare it to.

Boy! Claire Huxtable was so involved in her kids' lives, full of love and home-cooked meals! Mr. Huxtable was amazing as I watched him tell jokes to his kids and direct them on how to think and channel their emotions! Those kids were seen, heard, and seemingly loved!

I have an idea, I thought! "Mom, can you read us a bedtime story before bed tonight?"

Lol. I asked this question consistently for months! One time, I got a yes from her. Dad never gave a yes. My mind raced as disappointment began to settle in, and my heart began to drop. I began to wonder: am I important? Am I loved? Am I seen? From that moment on, I began investigating!

These things impact us as kids, and they can last year after year unless we recognize them as disappointments and address them through counseling, therapy, and prayer! Not necessarily in that order.

Another night with no dinner on the table? My parents were sitting at the bar in our living room. The white powder was in front of them while I sat under the kitchen table, watching them as I colored in my coloring book. I showed my pictures to them. "I drew you a picture, Daddy, Mama, look!" I proclaimed.

There was no response, just a slight glance. My head dropped as I thought, "I know they love me; let me try again."

"I drew you a picture, Daddy, Mama, look!" I repeated.

The response was the same every time. The white powder they sniffed was more important than what I was saying.

What is love? What does love mean?

Months later, I decided I was tired of guessing, so let me ask! "Daddy, do you love me?" The answer was, "No, but I like you." As he laughed, I didn't know what that meant.

"Mom! I asked Dad if he loved me, and he said no, but he liked me. What does that mean?"

Mama ignored me. I asked her three more times, and finally, out of frustration, she said, "I don't know!" Well, my final thoughts were that they didn't love me. Mama probably didn't know love because all Daddy ever did was beat her and tell her bad things about herself.

I guess love is only for certain people.

I am ten years old now, and my sister is five. The house is dark. It's quiet as my sister and I sit in our room, waiting to hear a car pull up or the front door open. If I hear that sound, maybe we will get to eat. It seems so late, and I'm hungry. Come on, sis, I have an idea!

My lunch kit is useful when it has food in it, lol. Let's walk across the street to 7-Eleven. Look, sis, the clerk is not here. I'm just going to load all this candy into our lunch kit! Sneakers, starbursts, ring pops, runts, rocky roads.... mmm- mmm...just keep looking to ensure no one comes!

Whew, we made it back home and didn't get caught! Now we could eat this and go to sleep. Stealing candy for dinner went on for months; finally, I got tired of stealing and felt so bad. As I walk down the hallway and turn right into my parents' dark bedroom, I feel my heart beating faster and faster. My thoughts are racing. Do you really want to do this? Will he notice? What will happen to Mama?

Surely, they can't expect us to go hungry every night. Daddy has tons of suits and keeps money inside one of these pockets: 300 dollars! I'm going to pay for our food tonight! The shopping is done, and I'll just put the change back in Dad's suit. I'm sure he will notice since there is a little change there, too.

YOU ARE A LIAR! I heard it being yelled the next day. Dad was mad and blamed Mom. Their bedroom door shut, and my heart dropped. As Dad was yelling and hitting Mom, I slowly walked to their door and stood there for a few minutes with my hand on the doorknob. My heart began to beat faster and faster. "Just open the door, Shema, and say, STOP HITTING MAMA"! That's what I told myself repeatedly.

I couldn't get the courage to do it. I was too scared, so I left and walked to a friend's house for about half an hour. My friends had no clue what I had to deal with almost every night.

Maybe I will try to cook something. Mom has a Betty Crocker cookbook! Maybe I can understand it, and the food will come out well! Hours later…well, it did not come out well; it was horrible and not edible! After months of trying, I realized cookies and cakes were the only thing I could make decently. So, I made it every week for me and my sister.

One day, after I made a batch of cookie dough, I decided to eat the dough! OMG, I was so sick that I threw up for half a day. Never again will I do that!

My sister was lucky. Dad would take her to school; on those days, he would buy her a McDonald's, but I couldn't figure out why he would feed her and not me. I guess it was because he didn't love me that much, or I wasn't important. Oh well, what can I do? Sometimes, parents do not see or pay attention to how their actions affect their kids. They seem to focus more on themselves.

Sometimes, they DO SEE but still don't say or do anything to help the kids' situation or change the outcomes. It's almost like adults are more important than kids. It is an unspoken expectation or understanding that kids should only do what they are told, not what they see or experience.

I wasn't supposed to be hungry! I wasn't supposed to see that Mom was abused, neglected, and exploited! I wasn't supposed to know I was neglected or my school clothes were not up to par!

A teacher in 4th grade told me one day, "Stop! Let me get a good look at you...your clothes actually match today." I remember thinking I'm not crazy. My school clothes are off! I was embarrassed; who else could see that my home life wasn't right? I was supposed to see that we owned a home, Dad had a motorcycle, a boat, two cars, a prestigious job, and vacations two to three times a year! Awesome stories to tell at school, right?

We ate more frequently on vacations but were still left alone so the adults could do their own thing. No one ever talked to us. It was just me and my younger sister. I felt like I had a kid to raise, but who would raise me? What am I supposed to do? Act like I see nothing?

Listen to track Sunshine (album Who Am I)

Chapter 1
Worksheet

Before starting these worksheets, it is required that you write each answer down! Do Not think of the answers only! Please write below each question!

1. What things were you told to look past?
Ex: man or woman touching you inappropriately, being used or lied to, abuse, etc.

2. What necessities were missing from your childhood?
Ex: food, housing, clothes, supervision, guidance, etc.

3. What did your parents/caregivers place as more important or valuable than you were?
Ex: another man or woman, another kid, money, material possessions, etc.

4. What adult responsibilities were placed on you as a child?
Ex: to work and provide for your family, care for other kids, perform intimate spousal duties, etc.

5. Describe your definition of what a healthy family looks like or should be like.

6. How young were you when you began to get an idea that something wasn't quite right?

7. What emotions do you remember having at ages:
Ex: I always felt fear, anxiety, confusion, alone, and worried.

Age 1

Age 2

Age 3

Age 4

Age 5

Age 6

Age 7

Age 8

Age 9

Age 10

Age 11

Age 12

Age 13

Age 14

(I had times of happiness as well!)

NOTE: Continue to the next chapter. The answers to these questions will make sense in later chapters as we dig deeper!

8. Write down how you should have felt as a child!

Chapter 2
Don't Say Nothing'

As much as we would like to think we are nothing like our failed parents, we are! We mimic their habits and tendencies many times without even trying. How they handle situations or not. How they speak to others or not. How we dress or not. How far do we go in education or not. There are always the exceptional few that break this mold, but for the most part, we are much like our parents.

Through reading this book and doing the worksheets, you will gain knowledge and the tools to use to change habits and outcomes for your future and the lives of your friends and loved ones.

Let's party! My parents liked parties, costume parties, birthday parties, just because parties, lol. Adults were drinking, cursing, smoking weed, cocaine, and who knows what else…As I skip around the party, I feel cigarette ashes drop on the top of my head. Ugh, an adult is not paying attention! I guess I have no reason to mention it other than it's a memory I have, lol.

There was a lot of sexual content floating in our atmosphere. Even though I didn't know much about sex, I knew it existed, and it must have been pretty important. No one spoke of it, but I guess I wasn't supposed to see, hear, or know about it and maybe not even speak about it.

I hear my parents arguing again as Dad's friends wait in the living room. Dad wants Mom's money, and she says, "That's all I have. If you take it, I won't have anything to eat for lunch at work." Dad didn't seem to care, so she gave it to him to avoid the beating.

Unfortunately, that meant I would worry all night and all day at school. I know how it feels to be hungry. I sat at school all day wondering if

Mom was okay. I hope she doesn't pass out. Maybe Dad's friend needed money, but why did he leave Mama hungry? He didn't care about Mama. It makes sense why she doesn't share anything with me or my sister. She's trying to hold on to what she can because Dad takes everything.

Again, I thought, "I don't want to be a girl."

Yeah, it hurts. No one gives it to anyone at my house. You have to figure out how to get your food and your stuff. Only the Huxtables and white people get love and care, or so I thought. At least Christmases and birthdays were good! Kinda. I never got anything I asked for, lol. Well, a few times, I got the Big Wheel bike I had asked for! Which seemed to always get stolen.

Sometimes, I wondered, would they even care if I got killed? I have an idea! Mom will be home in a little while. Sis, I have a plan! Lie down on the floor, and I will, too. Put this knife in between your armpit and side. We'll put ketchup around it, so it looks like someone killed us while they were gone so long. Hurry! I heard the car pull up! Lie down, lie down…

Mama walks in the door. She sees us as we lie quietly but doesn't say anything for a few minutes. Then she says, "Shema, Bianca, are you okay?" I laugh and jump up. "Mama, what if someone had killed us?"

She doesn't reply. I think if Mama wasn't so scared, and Daddy wasn't always beating on her, she would probably talk and play with us more. Sometimes, she would try to do special things with us, like have a movie night with chili cheese dogs AND popcorn! She would even talk to us, try to tell jokes, and make us laugh! I can count on one hand how many times that happened, though. Many nights, I would hear Mom saying, "No."

As I listen through my bedroom door, I know not to open it. I follow Mom's voice from the middle of my door to the floor. I'm trying to see under the door: why does it sound like she is on the floor? Her voice becomes distant. He dragged her out the front door. But why? I look out my window but don't see or hear anything. Is she dead? Will she come back? What do I do? What do I do with my sister? I don't know.

I've only heard rumors. The reason for her being dragged outside was so he could take pictures of her bruised and battered body and place them in a photo album to show all his friends and co-pimps what he could do. I remember when his friends would come over. He would make her stand in front of them while they looked at the pictures he had taken.

I didn't know what they were looking at, and every time I tried to look, Dad wouldn't let me. I knew something important in that book, but I never saw it. What a way to degrade and destroy a person's mind and self-esteem...but it is the seventies and eighties, and that's the way it is, at least in black households, I think. Mom has to give Dad every work check; she never sees her own money!

In 2023, I can't comprehend it. I guess that's what men and women experience with human trafficking. If she did not do as he said, she was beaten. Sometimes, Mom would talk about leaving Dad, and I would be happy. California, here we come!

I didn't know how to understand what was happening. Why was this happening?

Many times while my parents were gone, I did many things to occupy myself, but music was my real comfort! I would play 45s on the record player all day and sometimes at night: Michael Jackson, Ready for the World, Millie Jackson, Whispers, The Supremes, Curtis Blow, and Run DMC. I even won the talent show in the fifth grade! I sang Whitney Houston's "Greatest Love of All" at C.C. Ronnow Elementary School. A lot of the parents were there, but not mine.

Even though Dad was at home, he was lying in bed. I just did a quick run-through of my song for him, and he said, "It sounds good, but add your own style." It's okay. I just won't say anything – he's probably tired.

Always alone, I〉m getting used to it. Just say nothing. Today, after Mom got home from work, she actually began making dinner! Probably because Daddy wasn't home and wouldn't return until tomorrow. Lucky us!

Ring, ring... Mom and I answered the house phone at the same time. It was a man selling children's books. He asked Mom if he could speak with me alone on the phone. Mom said, "Hmm, ok," and hung up. I was just happy someone wanted to talk to me. What's your favorite cartoon? "Smurfs", I answered. Who's your favorite character? "Smurfette", I answered. Where's your mom? After we started laughing, he said, "I would like to come see you. Is that okay?"

Then the conversation changes to, "I will come to your bedroom window. When I knock, just open the window..." He heard my silence and hesitation, and said, "Trust me, it won't hurt. I will put some Vaseline on your butt, and it will feel good...." My response? "Ok." We hung up, and Mom asked me, "What did he say?"

I told her, "He told me not to tell you." Mom was upset and interrogated me until I told her. She called my dad. I didn't hear their conversation, and no one said anything after that. Was it bad? Was it okay?

What do I do when he shows up at my window? I was always nervous after that, even more so than before that happened. I guess you just don't speak about those things. Well, my parents are not home again. I have an idea! I know where they keep the weed! So, I climbed to my parent's waterbed, where they kept that old wooden box . I didn't smoke it, but I liked how it smelled, lol. I just smelled it and played with it a little. It didn't do much. I guess I'll watch TV....hmm, WHAT IS THIS?? PLAYBOY? SPICE? This doesn't look right. Is this what adults do? That looks like it hurts. Why are they doing that? At the same time, I'm having feelings I'm unsure about! It's supposed to feel good, but...I'm not supposed to feel this way. Is this right or wrong? I don't know, but I guess I won't say anything'. They don't answer me anyway.

Again, I don't want to be a girl... everything is difficult, and you are always on the losing end. No one cares about girls. A year or two later, on my birthday, I begged Mom for months to throw me a slumber party, and she said yes! All my friends came over: some cousins and my favorite aunt (the only aunt who actually listened to me). This was going to be the best birthday ever! We played in my room, eating snacks and drinks and having wrestling matches (I was a tomboy, lol).

I hear this hurling scream! "Aaaah, someone is at the window!" I stopped and looked; there was no one there. The bedroom window was open but had a screen on it. Mom came rushing into the room, and we told her everything was ok. When she left, we began wrestling again, having fun. "Aaaah, a man at the window! "

This happened several times: I stood at the window, seeing nothing. Then, finally, a Hispanic man popped up. He was ducking down under the window outside. I asked him, "What are you doing? Where did you come from? Where do you live?" He says, "Come outside; take the screen off so we can play." My crazy cousin Rosie takes her drink, throws it in his face, and starts yelling. Obviously, someone in her household was talking to her about safety!

Mom returns, and I tell her there's a man outside. I saw the true strength of my mom that night! While my aunt was by the phone ready to dial 9-1-1, Mom went outside to face a grown man alone! Wow, how did she get the courage to stand up like that? Maybe all the beatings she took from Dad had prepared her to fight men! Is that good or bad? Whatever it is, I'm proud of her and feel protected for the first time.

The man left. I believe he was our neighbor's son from across the street. He never came back! Unfortunately, as usual, my parents said nothing about the incident, although I believe they discussed it. I was left to always wonder...who is watching me? Who is out to get me? Who can see that hardly anybody is around? Who can see that I'm alone?

I spent a lot of time at my grandmother's house; she's always praying for me. I walk into the house, looking down the long hallway at the end of her bedroom. All the cousins and I knew you would always see her sitting with her door open, praying. When Grandma sees me, she says,

"Come here." She pours olive oil/anointing oil onto her hands, places it on my head, and prays in tongues (heavenly language) over me. I asked her, "Grandma, what are you saying? Who are you talking to?" She tells me, "I'm talking to the Lord." Grandma wasn't always fit to cook, but I knew I would get more meals with her than at home.

Grandma always had her front door open for anyone who needed food, encouragement, or a place to stay. There would be church luncheons and dinners. Sometimes, someone from the church would come to cook for her, or Grandma would take me to the Mainstreet Hotel and Casino buffet for dinner after church. My uncle Muhammad would tell me to stop eating so fast. "You act like you never ate before." They didn't know. I started to get used to people telling me that, although I didn't understand WHY they were telling me that.

My cousins from California came to visit Grandma one year. As I eat, I think, hopefully, I can get seconds. My cousin Kat says, "God! Stop eating like a pig; you act like you never ate before." I guess that's just how I eat; people will have to get used to it because I don't understand why they have a problem with how I eat.

Most of the time, when you come from a house filled with neglect, abuse, exploitation, and trauma, you will have habits that you are unaware of...but others can see it. What are the signs of a hungry person? (Me eating like a "pig" or very selfish with my food). What are the signs of a person who has lived in loneliness? (They can be clingy, show low self-esteem, be antisocial, over-talkative, passive-aggressive, or introverted). What are the signs of someone being abused or neglected? Poor hygiene, fearful, aggressive, timid, antisocial, multiple bruises, confusion, pain/discomfort, and disappearing for days at a time.

How do you have a healthy relationship with others when you can't see your own unhealthy flaws and the habits you have carried around for years? As I am now in my forties, I never received therapy, and no one ever mentioned that I was carrying a lot of baggage! Nor did anyone offer to help. Why not? Don't see nothing' and don't say nothing'! Is this right or wrong?

Mostly, family members will tell you to get help, but when you do, they will most likely talk about you and/or attempt to make you feel bad about it. Those people you have to overlook. They are the same ones who also held it in and "got past it" (passed it down to their kids and family). It usually shows up in the next generation if it doesn't destroy them first!

NOTE: The worksheets at the end of this chapter will help you identify some things and give you the tools to start working on yourself TODAY! The sooner you start, the brighter your future becomes. These habits and behaviors are called generational curses that can be handed down for centuries if someone in your family (you) doesn't step up to say No! I want something better for my life and the generations that are coming behind me.

It may have started with your grandparents, great grandparents, great, great grandparents, or somewhere further than that. It can range from molestation, incest, abandonment, alcohol or drug abuse, negative words or thoughts, behaviors, old or twisted mindsets, belief systems, culture, etc.

It took me a while to realize that many of my habits and my reputation were "Shema is mean; she can be a real bitch!" I had no filter in my mouth; my emotions were numb, and I was always ready to fight, steal, or diminish someone. I was mean to my little sister and treated her as Dad did Mom, minus the extreme abuse. My sister was sneaking, wearing my clothes to school because she felt alone, just as I did. She also wanted to have clothes that did not embarrass her at school. So, it seemed that my Mom, sister and I were all struggling to have something and be somebody while my father lived his best-facade life!

You would think I understood and had compassion toward my sister. I did not! I was not taught to have compassion, forgiveness, understanding, or love. Everything I learned was to take, be selfish, get your own, and nobody else matters. I just didn't have it to give. Of course, today, it still hurts my heart. I could not be a better sister, even though I knew it was not my fault. I also learned that siblings could take different paths despite growing up in the same dysfunctional house! For instance, in an alcoholic family, one brother/sister hates alcohol and never drinks, while the other brother/sister is a complete lush. My sister and I took different directions as well.

As I near the age of thirteen, I woke up for school...Mom has a black eye. I couldn't understand how an adult can do another adult like that, and it appears to be ok. What is this? I look at Mama and ask, "Mom, did you get a whippin'?" I wondered if this is another form of whippin' for adults.

If so, I don't want to be a girl. Mom didn't reply. I knew she was broken on the inside, even if she didn't say it. As I returned home from school, my sister and I sat on our bedroom floor, playing with dolls.

Quietly, I begin to pray, "God, why did you make me a girl? I don't want to be a girl. Do I have to live like this all my life? Can you change me or help me? I'm not special or important...God, I pray that you make me unique. Make me unique so when people see me, they will like me and love me and treat me good!" I prayed this prayer month after month, year after year, from seven to fourteen.

Sure, I doubted that God had heard me. I thought, why am I praying this like it's going to happen? I don't have anyone else to talk to; my only option is to pray. Maybe he is real, and maybe he will answer my prayer. Grandma told me to pray...I just will say nothing.

Questions! Why is a seven-year-old thinking this way or praying that hard at such a young age? How does a seven-year-old use such a big word so early? UNIQUE? I never told anyone about that prayer until I hit my forties. I look back and think, wow! How did I make it without being molested or kidnapped or something worse?

Listen to track: I Wonder "album- I Am"

Chapter 2
Worksheet

Before starting these worksheets, it is required that you write every answer down! Do Not think of the answers only! Please write below each question!

1. How did you view your gender as a child?
Ex: Did you regret being a boy or girl?

If so, why? If not, Good for you!

2. What was the one consistent message being played at your house?
Ex: Everything belongs to dad/mom; it's only good if mom says it is (like Bobby Bushay on "Water Boy" LOL), you're unlovable, etc.

Whatever the message (s) was! It is a lie! It is, more than likely, still causing you problems today! Now, take some time and write down the opposite of that message! Write the truth of the matter!

Repeat this truth to yourself every day!!!

3. What activities did you fill your time or mind with as a kid?
Ex: cooking, music, sports, school, drawing, writing, dreaming, etc.

4. Did you feel protected as a child? If so, by whom?

5. How often was this person around?

6. What percentage of the time did you feel safe?
Ex: 10% of the time? 30%, 50%, 80% etc.

7. List the flaws and faults of which you are aware!
Ex: drinking, drugs, sex, bullying, overeating, lying, etc.

8. Have you ever had professional therapy or counseling?

If so, did it help? If not, why not? If you went to therapy without help, I encourage you to try again! Sometimes, you must go through a few to find the right one! Like finding a good doctor or barber.

9. What were some things you did not understand about your family while growing up?

10. Did you have siblings?

If so, did anyone duplicate the offense?
Ex: abuse, neglect, exploiting others, lies, deceit, etc.

Did any of the siblings do the opposite of the offense?

11. Did you grow up in church?

If not, what did you depend on to help you cope? If so, did you pray?

What were your prayers? It is important to remember these and write them out! They are still active and working in heavenly places. Grasp them and write them now! Were any of those prayers answered? If so, how many were answered?

12. What things can you look back on and see where someone or something saved you from going through more? Write them below!

Chapter 3
I Don't Understand

It's the weekend! I hear Mom fussing with Dad because she wants to visit family. I hope we get to go...yes! On our way to Big Mama's house (my grandmother), I see more cars; it looks like my aunts and uncles are here too! I might get to play with my cousins! As we walk through the front door, my sister takes off to the back of the house, where the kids usually go, but I stop, sit on the floor, and try to comprehend what I am looking at. Mom, Aunt Chilly, and Aunt Brenda all have black eyes. I don't understand. So, this is what men do to women? I want to hear how this happens or what this is!

They did not speak about it much as I sat there. I wonder, "Mom has brothers, so why don't they defend their sisters?" Maybe brothers and men don't protect women. Is it an unspoken rule? As I thought, my uncle said, "We can blow his boat up!" I thought, "Yes! He does want to defend his sister... But, well, what would that do?" I guess it scared my dad. I guess the cousins were also used to it, as none of them tried to find out what was happening, and neither was my sister.

So many things do not make sense to me. All I know is that I no longer want to be a girl. No one protects you; they only take from you, and girls are nobody. I thought maybe my Big Mama was hurt to see three of her girls with black eyes. Maybe I would see a reaction from her that said, "Let's do something about this," but I realized there was no reaction to expect...this must be normal.

Maybe Grandmother was treated badly by men; in return, she may be treated men badly, too (my dad). In return, he treated his wives and girls badly. Is this the generational curse that plagues my family? I know one thing for sure! I did not treat my boys or daughters that way. I chose to break that curse!! I treated my boys like princes and my daughter like a princess. They know NOTHING of abuse, neglect, being hungry, unloved, unseen, or unheard. This brings me peace, joy, and solace.

I wasn't a perfect mother, but the proof is in the pudding! Over the years, multiple people have asked me, "Shema, how did you get your kids like that?" Depending upon their situation with their kids, I gave different answers, but the real answer is to break the curse – the family/cultural routine!

What is your family culture? Be seen, not heard? Do as you are told. Don't say anything? Unstable jobs? Incest? Multiple abortions, drugs, alcohol, neglect? Name it., then pray about it! Give it to the Lord Jesus, and then take action! It may not sound like the best or real answer, but trust me, it is! I can only tell you how I made it through and gave my kids a different direction and a better life. If you don't know God, here is how you meet him! Say this aloud!

Lord of all creation, Heaven and Earth, I don't know you, but I heard you can help me. I would like to get to know you. You made me and put me on this earth for a reason. You gave me the parents you gave me for a reason. I don't understand any of my life. It's painful, disappointing, and discouraging. I have habits and behaviors that only get me into trouble.

I ask you, Jesus, to please come into my heart and show me who you are. Forgive me for all of my wrongdoings and my sins. I believe you are the son of God and that you died on the cross for me so my life would be better here on earth and after I leave this earth. Come into my heart and teach me your ways of love, prosperity, kindness, meekness, gentleness, generosity, gratitude, long-suffering, healing, AND my purpose in life.

It is just that simple! Now get your hands on a Christian bible: King James or New King James. The NIV is easier to understand or starts with a children's bible. As you begin to read and pray daily, you will begin to feel God's presence (the Holy Spirit), and your thoughts, emotions, and reactions will also change in an unexplainable way! He is alive and real; he will answer your prayers.

Next, get a journal! Begin writing in it daily. There is something about seeing it on paper versus holding it in your mind. Trust me! You can track your growth and changes this way. Plus, when God begins to speak to you and reveal things, it's nice to look back and remember things you may have forgotten!

I don't quite understand how God does these things, like healing your heart or changing the way you think. My conclusion is that he is real because it works!!

My sister and I were always caught in the middle. Mother later told me the final straw was when I asked her, "Mom, did you get a whooping?" See, I was still trying to figure this thing out, lol! Mother decided that it was time to leave. Of course, Dad was not in agreement.

As I sat in class the next day, my third-period teacher pulled me out of class and took me to the office. "You have visitors". I don't know these people. They begin asking me about my parents. Long story short, it's Child Protective Services... Why are these people here? I just could not understand. Why would Dad want Mom to stay when he treats her so badly? It must be love; if you love someone, you want them to stay. This went on for a few years, back and forth. You know, CPS is coming around.

Dad won the divorce; he got the house, all the cars, boats, motorcycles, etc., that Mom helped pay for with her work check that she never saw. It was like watching someone take all her strength, resources, energy, and life away and then leave her to dwindle.

I didn't understand, nor did I have anything to say. We moved, and Dad bought an apartment complex. We moved into one of the units for a while... maybe things will get better now. Unfortunately, nothing has changed: no food, love, attention, or supervision. He was still gone a lot. He had a new girlfriend and spent the night at her place often, or she was at our place, or he was at work.

Music was still my comfort, and my little sister was still in her own world... wherever that was. As I open the front door of our new apartment, I feel the fresh air gently brushing my face as a slightly cool breeze tickles my nose. I put on an album by Midnight Star (slow jam). I would sing that song over and over, lol!

I heard the dog outside barking but didn't think anything of it. As I continue to sing, the barking becomes louder AND more aggressive. I step out the front door, and a white man is trying to get up the stairs into our apartment! Dad is not around. I don't know this guy, but the dog is set on stopping him! My sister was so naive then that she thought she was trying to save the dog from the man! As I yell at her, "Stop, let the dog go", she won't listen to me. Luckily, the dog wouldn't listen to her! The neighbors downstairs hear the commotion, come outside, and make the man leave. I was so thankful. I don't think I'm as strong as Mom is to challenge a grown man!

Who left me with this kid, anyway!! I told Dad later when he got home, but he said nothing. I don't understand why I am stuck raising my sister. Who is going to raise ME, I thought. A few days later, we were at the grocery store (Albertson's), and I saw the white man sitting, playing slots. I pointed him out to my dad, but he just looked and again said nothing. A fresh reminder that girls are unimportant, and no one will stand up for you...except for my dog and Mom. I guess the nice neighbor guy downstairs, too.

So many things I don't understand. What I have learned up until the age of fourteen is that sex drives people, and the best thing to do is not say anything and take what's given to you. That incident only added to my fear, anxiety, nervousness, decreased self-esteem, and more.

I sometimes wonder if Mom met Dad at seventeen when he was twenty-seven. How did her mind, body, emotions, and mentality develop if she had never fully developed? She started an abusive relationship for thirteen years, from age seventeen to her thirties... interesting thought!

What's more interesting is that I can't remember ever having a "mother." I saw glimpses of what she could be to me and my sister. She had it in her to love me, maybe share her food with me, even play with me. That is something I have experienced very little of to this day.

However, I clearly remember some of the dysfunctional things Dad would say to me about Mom as I sat in the bed with my parents watching TV. "Go make something to eat," Dad told Mom. As she walks away, Dad tells me, "Always wear a bra. You don't want your boobs looking like that." I sat looking at Mama, walked away, and thought, "I don't know much about boobs, but I do want nice ones. That was mean." I don't want to be a girl: this is too hard and unhappy. I remember the feeling of having a responsibility to tell Dad things about Mom.

Later, Mom tells me I was brainwashed and manipulated by Dad to be a liar. Maybe that's part of why I never felt right on the inside. Who knows?

As children, it's easy to think we are the problem with our parents. Like we are a burden: if we change or leave, things will be better, not understanding that it is not us! It is not the kids; it's the baggage our parents carry from their childhood, from our grandparents! They did not get therapy or counseling. They were taught, "Don't see nothing, don't say nothing, deal with it". Your parents may not know how to love or receive love and may not know how to share or care. They can only give you what they know or have experienced themselves.

As I mentioned, many cultures and people of lower socioeconomic status do not believe in counseling or sharing with others that they need help. You don't want to appear "weak," so the generational curses usually continue.

I can only imagine, if a girl felt this way, how do boys feel when they are belittled, emasculated, molested, neglected, etc? Could this be the same reason many boys don't want to be boys? Why do girls turn to girls and boys turn to boys? I do praise God that I did not have to drink from the cup of homosexuality, although many do! We all take different routes to find a safe space where we feel protected, accepted, AND loved.

The worksheets in this chapter will guide you to some answers and revelations you may have been unaware of. Take your time; processing this information will not be a one-day thing! It may take weeks, months, or years to really grasp the depth of all that has happened to you and how to get free. Understanding comes with patience and a willingness to listen and be truthful with yourself!

If you have found yourself in homosexuality or some other form of pain relief that is unhealthy or questionable, I encourage you to begin your journey to healing. Your choices should not be based on pain, disappointment, fear, anxiety, dysfunctional childhood manipulation, or your past. That decision should be made from a healthy, healed place.

Recite the prayer above in Chapter 2 and ask God to reveal to you and deliver you from anything attached to you when you were too young to know better or understand what was taking place. Ask him to set your feet on solid ground! 2 Cor. 10:5.

The Bible says it is better that a man be drowned at the bottom of the ocean than to touch one of his little ones. (Luke 17:2) There is love for you. I didn't understand it for many years. GOD IS LOVE! WHERE, you ask?

God is love! I will explain this in the following chapters. He sees it all, hears it all, and is protecting you somewhere in your story! While he will not make your life perfect, he will use your trauma to prepare you for your calling to help others!

Draw closer to God; his presence alone will change your circumstances! Learn to bring his presence into your home (the Holy Spirit)!! I couldn't see it for a long time, but as I write this book, I can only do so because God brought some things to my attention! He did some unexplainable work in my life! Does it still hurt when I think about it? Sometimes.

Do I understand my parents' upbringing and their flaws? Yes. Are they excused from their choices and behaviors? No. Have I forgiven them?

Yes. What I have learned is that we all have flaws or sins (lying, stealing, cheating, murder, rape, etc.) No one gets to have a perfect life! It's what you do with it that matters! Have you ever heard the saying, "When life gives you lemons, just make some lemonade!" Get it?

Things to get you started: write a book, start a support group, initiate a phone hotline or social media page for those going through what you've gone through or are going through right now! Locate a trustworthy person to help you develop a plan, get therapy, and lead others to therapy. Watch God bring healing, resources, finances, true friendships, support, love, and more through your decision to take your lemons and make lemonade!

Sometimes, you don't have to understand; just stay focused on overcoming the issue and follow the steps!! You are young, but you have power! You have a voice! You are loved! You are not alone; you have unseen strength through Jesus Christ! 2 Cor 12:9-10.

Chapter 3
Worksheet

Before starting these worksheets, it is required that you write every answer down! Do Not think of the answers only! Please write below each question!

1. Can you identify one or more curses passed down through multiple generations of your family?
Ex: alcoholism, drug abuse, molestation, lying, manipulation, faking, materialism, etc.

Once you have identified these things, think about what you can do to change these things for the next generation! We will also pray about these in a later chapter. If you are unsure about how many generations there are, ask the elders in your family and research your grandparents, great-grandparents, parents, cousins, aunts, uncles, etc. You will find a root somewhere!

2. What is the culture of your family? Mom's/dad's side.
Ex: fake it till you make it? Drink AND smoke at every gathering? Leave the kids while the adults go away? Etc.

I have TWO cultures. One side of my family is bougie/uppity, educated, selfish, secretive, extra! LOL The other side is Urban, down to earth about that life! LOL. Either way, they both drink a lot and like to party!

3. Do you know what your purpose in life is? If so, write it below!

If not, do you know how to find out? Yes or no?

4. Have you ever journaled before? Yes or no?

If not, congratulations! If you have been completing the worksheets, you have been journaling! Journaling helps you to keep track of the changes you go through each year and the prayers you have prayed, along with the prayers that have been answered! Journaling can help you find your way when you get off track! Journal daily!!! It's good for your mental health!

5. Do you want to see change take place within yourself? If not, stop reading this book! If yes, write below what you would like to see change!
Ex: attitude, behavior, ways of thinking, etc.

6. Do you struggle with believing in God? If yes, why? If not, write below why you have been stuck in this same cycle for so long. (for adults only). Have you ever submitted this issue to the Lord before?

7. Can you take hearing the truth about yourself?

8. Are you able to be honest with yourself about yourself?
If not, learn to get to that place! If you can't see It or accept it, you can't change it!

9. Do you believe that your life and how you feel right now can change? If no, why not? If yes, you are in a good place! Write the answers below!

10. What steps will you or can you take to solve the problem of your current situation?
Ex: Get past your fear? Speak up more? Find a trustworthy person. Etc.

11. What will your lemonade be?
Ex: support group? Social media help page? Etc.

Chapter 4
Don't Know What You Don't Know!

Von Tobel Middle School witnessed some of the roughest years of my life. Now I'm fourteen years old, smoking weed, starting my "menstrual cycle," boobs coming in, no self-esteem, and hungry! No Mom to be found. So, do you know what that means for my sister and me? Crazy hair, crazy clothes, a dry, smelly, and bald street! I had a "Jerry curl" at that time (eighties)! If you've ever watched the original movie "Coming to America" with Eddie Murphy, just think of the guy with a "soul glow"! only I didn't have the glo!! I never made it to the beauty shop on time. Sometimes, I would get braids. I can't even remember how my sister's hair was so unkempt!

Here is a story I will share with you   . There were these two black girls that really picked on me all the time. They were dark-skinned, and I am light-skinned (not always the best mix). It always seemed like in every school I attended, it was always a dark-skinned girl who wanted to pick on me... anyhow, one of the girls at lunch would sneak up behind me when I was eating and dump her plate on my head with ketchup and barbecue sauce in my SHORT and already DRY unkempt hair!

This went on for months. I would go home and try to clean it, but as light-skinned as I am, I did not get the "good" hair! LMBO!! My hair would nap up. We had no hair dryer. I did not know how to do my hair. Many times, I wouldn't even wash it. Someone says yuck! One day, one of the most popular boys at school walked past me and said,

"Ugh, her hair stinks!" Yes! He said it! I Heard it but hoped no one would notice. Some would ask: why didn't you tell the teachers or your parents about the girls at school?

Honestly, 1. I did tell the school twice, but they did nothing. Finally, they stepped in on the third or fourth visit to the office. 2. I knew Dad wouldn't care or probably wouldn't say anything. The second girl? Well,

I used psychology on her! You see, neglect, and I had gotten so close that I could see it in other people after a while.

I could see she felt ugly, unloved, unseen, and unheard, plus she was overweight and probably felt bad about her skin tone as well. So, I asked her on the bus, "Do you have a boyfriend?" She answered, "No." I said, "Oh, I thought you had all the boys. You're so pretty." Do you know that girl never bothered me again!!??? Lol

Now, back to my hair, lol! It was very rare that my hair, clothes, or mind were kept up. I could only take a bologna sandwich and an orange for lunch. Breakfast usually consisted of Raisin Bran cereal or oatmeal. I continued trying to learn how to cook; it was a hard challenge! My cousin, Rosie, would give me some of her lunch tickets at school so I could eat something different sometimes. Most of the time, I would pack bologna and throw it away when I got to school. I was so tired and embarrassed of repeating and eating the same simple foods.

Dad is at his girlfriend's house again. We were stuck in the house, but the girlfriend has a son who drives! Now I can be a little bit mobile, hopefully! As her son comes around more often, I immediately notice he is nice. He is quite different from the people I'm used to! What is this? He is nice. Nonjudgmental, helpful, slightly compassionate. Where do they make these people? I can actually talk to him. Interesting…he knows things…. hmm…. things I'm supposed to know, but I don't know what I don't know. I always felt like everyone in class was smarter than me. Like they knew things, I didn't know.

It took me a while to figure out what that was, but I know now! He was raised by parents or at least one parent. He was taught how to think, and he had knowledge and understanding; he also had confidence… wow, how did he get that??

Long story short, his hormones were in full effect, and my little fourteen years had already prepared me for more. I guess he could look past the greedy, short, smelly-haired girl and see something else, lol! I had no reason to say no… I don't recall anyone ever teaching me to say no. I guess you don't know what you don't know. At least my first time was with a nice guy!

More dysfunction, you say? Ah, but yes! My whole life has been dysfunctional up until this point. It wouldn't be right to change it now! Yes, our parents found out and flipped their lids! As crazy as this may sound, I could never understand why Dad was so upset. He was never around; he didn't feed us right or keep us as girls should be kept. He didn't talk to us besides making commands. We just sit in the house every day! My sister at least went to Girl Scouts after school (sometimes), and now he wants to act like he cares. Did I miss something? Is his anger caring, love, or is it selfishly motivated? I don't know! Do you?

ome decisions you have been making (starting from the age you started experiencing trauma and disappointments) stemmed from the conclusions you came up with when you didn't even realize you were having emotions (abandoned, lonely, frequently disappointed, etc.). You were too small to know. We can only remember moments of our lives. You can remember a happy, frustrating, or maybe a sad moment. Example: If you were thinking of a memory when you were three years old. Do you remember when your aunt took your candy because you wet yourself? That was one moment in June of 2001.

Do you remember what happened every other day, hour, minute of June 2001 (pick a year)? Do you remember all of it? No, you don't! So, in those spaces, you don't remember, believe it or not, you were having emotions and learning habits even if they were not traumatic moments. We have learned behaviors: some good, some not so good. So, what lies are you believing about life? About yourself? About your upbringing or your parents, which replay in your mind repeatedly?

We are old enough now to look back and say, "Hmm, Mom missed it on that, or Dad missed it on that." (name your caregiver in the place of your mom or dad). So, what did they teach me here or didn't teach me there? I can take it and change my view and/or let it go! It was never true or correct. This simple exercise may lead to being truly able to forgive your offender!

The worksheets in this chapter will help you identify the reasoning or emotions behind specific decisions you have made or are still making! Now is the time to recognize and work on those hurts and offenses. If you were an infant or toddler at the time of the trauma or incident, some behaviors or habits you may not be aware of due to lack of memory.

Again, you want to make informed decisions outside of a good, healthy place. Not out of hurt, anxiety, depression, or disappointment. We can't escape learning how to be an "adult". As I am now fifteen, turning sixteen, CPS has placed us back with our mom. Let's see how this goes! We definitely had more food and school lunches. Mama tried to keep up with our hair; she tried taking us shopping every four to five months. This was different! I saw another side of her: jewelry and eating at restaurants frequently. She talked to us more and laughed with us more. It was cool.

This is Chapter 4; dear reader, you should know by now that dysfunction hasn't stopped in my life yet! Long story short, as I now live with my mother, I gradually find out that my best friend's dad hooked up with my mom, and the nightmare begins! My best friend's dad was married and had numerous kids. My best friend, Icy, quit being my friend! She couldn't take the scandal. It might have been for the best because her dad was a liar! Nothing but problems all through our family. I guess I couldn't expect anything less.

Another level of hurt and disappointment looms. I'm not heard, I'm not seen, I'm not important. Adults come first; kids come last! Does that sum it up? Many more things happened that I am not including in this book. Hopefully, you get the picture!

Your foundation sets the course for your life! What is your foundation? What story was told to you as a child growing up with your family/ caregivers? Was it dysfunctional? If yes! Congratulations, you have issues! You need therapy, whether you believe it or not!

Most likely, you are making decisions that are not beneficial to you, whether you believe it or not! You will have difficult relationships if you do not address them starting today! These issues can hinder you financially, emotionally, mentally, spiritually, and physically. Don't wait until you get into your twenties, thirties, and forties. Start now and take control of your destiny!

If not, you still have issues, lol!   Just not as bad. These are things that the future me would tell the past me if I could go back in time! Let him, who has ears to hear, listen. (Matt. 11:15)

I made many bad decisions out of lack and neglect. At fourteen or fifteen, I already decided that it would be cool if I got pregnant. What's wrong with this thinking? Thank God I didn't get pregnant until I was nineteen! I can tell you it was a miracle because I was not using protection! WHAT? It was the eighties and nineties, and no one used protection. I don't think they did, lol! Baby R. Kelly was Poppin', NWA, Too Short, Baby Face, L.L. Cool J, New Edition, and some! Condoms? Protection? What!? You trippin', lol...

God is good, though!   He spared me from my ignorance. Again, I didn't know what I didn't know! I wanted someone to love and love me and possibly a way to leave home early. Maybe I was a repeat of my mother's situation when she went home. Who knows, but God knew I would struggle. I didn't have a life that would have completely knocked it down.

Adults are called adults for a reason. An adult is meant to represent maturity. However, those two words are not interchangeable. Just because a person is labeled an adult doesn't mean they are mature, trustworthy, responsible, or dependable. A person can be very mature age-wise and not be an adult at all.

I recommend watching the movie Matilda! This movie perfectly depicts how a super-intelligent, compassionate child can be born from parents who are quite the opposite! Matilda also reveals how positive things can come out of the ugliest places if you focus on your dreams and find someone you can trust.

You have it easy right now because you are reading this book! I did not have a dream to focus on. There was too much name-calling and degrading taking place in my home and a great lack of support! That's why I considered having kids instead of going to college.

We can't control who births us; we can't control our caregivers, and we can't force people to love us, see us, or hear us the way we need to be. You can control your choices to be different and make a difference. You can control if you have a personal relationship with Christ as a resource with everlasting help! Think of him as "the everlasting Gobstopper" from the Willy Wonka movie with Johnny Depp, lol!!!

He is a comforter; he does hold the answer and will never leave nor forsake you! We mostly feel like no one is listening, anyway, so you have all the time to get to know the Holy Spirit in a real way! The only one who will listen anytime, anywhere, for however long! Do you want to be Loved? He knows who is right for you!

To be seen/heard? He knows which doors to open for you and which ones to close. Restoration? You will be surprised at how God will restore things that were lost or stolen from your childhood to you. It will be in a way that you never thought.

Try it! You have nothing to lose and everything to gain!

Sixteen years old, now I see some of my older cousins with black eyes. I am convinced that this is how this thing goes! I still don't want to be a girl, though, and it's starting to sink in now. I date guys, but I don't ask for anything my cousins tell me I should. The guys are supposed to buy me things... I was never comfortable doing so. I always felt like I'd rather get my stuff and do my own thing financially. I mean, sometimes, they buy me things and take me out. Looking back, it was not on the level I would have charged ! I didn't know what I didn't know! Hey, men don't take care of women, is what I was taught and thought. You have to get your own! My brain had been on repeat from that message for over forty years!

Until today, Mom refuses to let a man have their name on her house! Not even her husband! Why?? She had to get her own, and no one else will take away what she worked for again! My sister is stuck on that message as well. Hmm. See how simple that was, yet troublesome? How can I have the habits of a selfish male, a passive woman, and be in a relationship with a man? Or vice versa if you are a male? It can go many ways depending upon the habit or behavior placed in your foundation.

Back to choices: I chose guys who were no good for me. I didn't know it at the time! All I saw was that we matched. We both struggled. We both stole what we needed. We both had to chop it up or "take it to the chest." We were always broke or hustling. We had common ground.

Some would argue we did not! This next statement discredits the argument that people with money and resources don't have struggles like those in projects or trailer parks! I am living proof! Lol. How do kids living in an apartment complex not have home-cooked meals every day? How do they walk around with nappy, unclean hair? How do they never have money in their pockets for school lunch? How is it that they only get three outfits per school year?

Ok, well... maybe it was a little better than the projects. We did get three outfits instead of one or none, but I still had to beg family members for shoes. Hold up! No, it wasn't better; the kids in the projects were showing up with Jordans, K-Swiss, Diadora, Converse, Adidas, etc. How do they look like they live in the suburbs, and I look like I came straight from the hood?

I know what it feels like not to want to open your mouth to ask the offender for one penny or have your peers ask why you look or dress a certain way. Why do your parents not do this or don't do that for you? For years, it would cut, and the older I got, the deeper it cut. I still get that question to this day! Only it doesn't cut me now... It's just embarrassing, and I choose not to re-educate others on it. Now they can just read my book! In short, I say childhood trauma!

Think of the movie "Mommy Dearest". If you haven't seen it, watch it! This is the perfect depiction of my childhood in a sense. The mother was a famous actress with two children. She only did things for them to make herself look good. Her daughter struggled financially in college and asked for money to help her get by for the month. Her mom said, "No it's better for you to do it all on your own." She trained her daughter to work hard for other people instead of training her to be a boss or entrepreneur as she was. As long as the mother had what she wanted, she didn't care about anything or anyone else, including her children. The daughter was confused; she had been trying all her life to figure out what love was and if what her mother was showing her was true and trustworthy. It was never about the kids; it was all a facade. Maybe, in some way, the mother did love her children.

How can a child take that as love? Do you think that is love? Or not? How does a child of a movie star not have the same knowledge/ resources as the parent or a similar mindset as the parent?

The only thing Mommy Dearest ever spoke to her children about was how to conduct themselves and get an education and a job! There were no scenes where Mommy Dearest sat the kids down during negotiations or signing contracts. So, that's exactly what the kids did; they continued to struggle and work at their jobs while holding hurt toward Mommy dearest. Great movie, though, lol!

These types of movies are true for some people, such as myself! My parents never spoke to me about owning a business, although I watched Dad for years as he started multiple enterprises. When I went to a family reunion, one of my father's cousins, Jay, asked, "Why don't you have a business yet? You are supposed to own a business already!" As I'm listening to her speak, I'm thinking at the same time, "Why don't I have a business? Why have I never thought of this? Dad never told me I was supposed to own a business. He suggested a beauty salon, but…" I was twenty-eight to thirty years old at that time!

I hesitantly answered her, "I don't know. What kind of business? How do I start one?" She definitely had my attention! From there, I began to pray and seek knowledge on how to do this! I realized the broken record still playing in my foundation was that only Dad gets everything. We only get what he tells us we can have. Everyone is dumb, but Dad. Don't ask for anything because you're not getting it unless its Christmas time... and that's a maybe! Are you in such a situation? You can't depend on your caregivers?

Trust is broken and gone, with no support system? Don't know what love really is? Everything is blurry and uncertain. People think you're crazy, a lost cause. See, It doesn't matter if your family is financially capable of doing better or NOT. It doesn't matter if they have the knowledge or resources to set your life on an amazing path or NOT! It doesn't matter if they see you as a legacy or a burden. They just may not do it for whatever reason or no reason!

Regardless of one's socioeconomic status, our issues are the same, and the solutions are the same! Make sure of this as you complete and end this journey with me. When you raise your children or loved ones, a legacy is what you will choose to leave behind in someone else – not baggage, simple material objects, or cultural norms!

What do you want to be remembered for? Your past trauma and habits (lemons) or you're redefined, new you (lemonade)? No, you're not crazy! Work through this book and see where it lands you from here!

Remember: You are never too old to start your journey to healing! NEVER

Listen to track: In His Presence (part 2) {Album I Am}

Chapter 4
Worksheet

Before starting these worksheets, it is required that you write each and every answer down! Do Not think of the answers only! Please write below each question!

1. What have you been living in for so long that now you can recognize it in other people?
Ex: abuse, neglect, loneliness, shame, etc.

2. What are the lies (lie) you have been believing about yourself?
Ex: I'm dumb, I'm ugly, I'll never be anything special, I'm unlovable, no one likes me, etc.

3. What is the truth?

4. Have you been trying to figure out what love is?

5. Have you ever experienced love before?

6. What is your definition of love?

7. What is society's definition of love?

8. What is god's definition of love

9. Do you know how to receive love? If no, why not? Write it below.

10. What makes you feel loved?
(your answers will not be the same as others)

11. Are you able to give love to others? If no, why not?

12. Who are you still holding a grudge against? Why?

13. After reading this chapter, do you look at that person(s) slightly different?

If so, what changed your perception? If you do not see them differently yet, continue reading the next chapters.

14. How often have you moved from house to facility or facility to facility?

15. How many childhood offenses have you had to endure? One? Two? More?

16. Did you work through those offenses or bury them as if it never happened?

17. Can you describe what your foundation is? Write it below.

Your foundation is the eyeglasses that you view life through. Is your foundation a rejection? Inferiority? Narcissism, etc. For me, it was "girls are not important, and I'm on my own.

18. Describe a time you made a bad choice but were spared!

19. What legacy do you want to leave behind on this earth? What will you be remembered for??

Chapter 5
Does Truth Exist?

The common understanding (those who have been mistreated) we all have is trust issues! Broken trust usually doesn't start with a one-time offense (although it can). It's usually repeated experiences that develop over a short or long period. Let me tell you my story of trying to establish what truth and trust are!

I was one or two years old when my parents and I were at Uncle Elbert's house. He had a big swimming pool in the backyard! He used to play basketball for UNLV, the local university in Las Vegas. I sat on the side of the pool, watching Dad jump in and out of the pool from the diving board. Then I had an idea ! Lol. I wondered, "If I jump in this pool, will he come get me? I can't swim, but Daddy loves and will get me. I think, then, I know I can trust him! But how much can I trust him? Will he see me and get me?

Okay... I will jump in the next time he jumps in, too! 1...2...3... oops! I'm not ready, LOL... so one more time! He is coming up, and I'm jumping in. NOW! Hear me! I was only one- or two years old testing this! As I float downward, I remember thinking, "Did he see me? How long can I hold my breath before I can't anymore? Will Dad get me? Will I die?" I sat at the bottom of the pool and waited and waited! Obviously, he came and got me because I'm talking to you now! Lol... This is just one moment I can remember from July of one year.

We start early, establishing who we can trust, what is the truth, what is good, what is right, and how this all works! We naturally want to be loved, nurtured and taught. That is the way God made us because he IS love! (1 John 4:8). The problem starts when our caretakers break the trust. Maybe it was lies told on a regular, maybe it was a physical offense, or maybe they just did not protect you when you knew they could protect you.

Luckily, Dad got me out of the pool. That established a form of trust. He wouldn't let me die! We can both agree that over time, you simply learn to trust people to be exactly who they are. That is the conclusion I came to year after year with my parents. They are who they are, and they will never change. That's not to say no one will change, but don't expect it! If it happens, great, but I watched my sister try for decades to change my father's perception of his children and how he viewed women; it broke her down every time! She tried using love, she tried simple conversations, and she tried literally cursing him out! Finally, she realized she just wasn't going to get the ear, love, or sincerity she yearned for from him, and she quit trying. As our elders would tell her, "Suck it up, get passed it, and stay quiet!" Interpretation: hold on to your hurts and trauma. You don't need healing. You are too old, and we won't help you either.

These responses only come because they were told the same things and did the same things with their traumas. Again, it passes to the next generation! For African Americans, this is the old slavery survival mindset. This mindset does not and will not work in today's society. Does truth exist? Yes! How do you know what truth is and what it is not? Can I trust the truth?

When we are confused about so many things in our lives, it can make us feel stupid! People say one thing, then do another. How do you find trust or truth in that? Growing up, I did not know how to tell if the information I was receiving or hearing was something I could use confidently, whether it was a universal truth that everyone agreed with or a lie.

After all, living in my household, all I saw was arguing, degrading, fighting, and lacking. Plus, at school, it seemed like everyone was smarter than me. Mom was convinced that I was a liar. I heard the words "dummy, stupid" so much at my house that I thought it was the hottest song on the top billboard! I was not the most outspoken because I had no confidence in what would come out of my mouth, or… should I say, out of my mind!

Most of the time, I would say things, and my peers or family would correct me because it wasn't right. I just wanted to know what everyone else knows that I don't. How do my friends know things? How do they know how to do things in order? Even if it was as simple as cooking or using products. I thought my brain was empty, and I just had to come up with something! I would think, "How do they know this stuff? How do I get to learn it?"

Truth: parents/caregivers should provide you with love, acceptance, security, stability, encouragement, support, guidance, necessities (food, shelter, water, clothes), knowledge, and wisdom.

Truth: All parents/caregivers come from different backgrounds, eras, and experiences. In the 1940s, it was okay for a thirty-five-year-old man to marry a thirteen-year-old girl and start having kids. It was okay for the man to beat his wife and cheat. Society accepted it. This is the era your great-grandparents probably came from. I have one aunt who was married at fourteen or fifteen years old. In her era, it was approved. This is the reason my mother was able to marry at the age of seventeen. This may also be the reason my father thought it was okay to abuse my mother.

In my parents' time and the new era, they did NOT find it okay to marry me off at thirteen, fourteen, fifteen, or even eighteen! (praise God)   , although I do not believe Daddy thinks it is okay to beat on women now! I don't believe he would want to see that happen to me, even though he had to endure seeing one of his girls go through an abusive relationship.

Again, he never says anything about it. As for my era, I wouldn't let a male or female put their hands on my children without speaking up, stepping up, and being very vocal about how my children and legacy are to be treated. Marriage? I have taught them to recognize signs and think with wisdom and understanding. They must first understand who they are (identity), then choose wisely who fits their purpose and calling. If you look at it from the perspective of an era, it doesn't excuse the behavior, but it helps you understand how some caregivers make their decisions.

Some may not have been very educated; some caregivers were abused, neglected, and abandoned themselves. They could only give what they had to give, even if it was really shitty! For this reason, we must forgive and let go. Forgive them because they didn't know better. Forgive because, just like you, they were trying to figure out how to deal with their past offenses and move forward, but they never found out how. Forgive them because they didn't know what they didn't know!

These are hard truths. I had to swallow this pill, also! Let it go! My parents did not have the wisdom or thought processes I had. Whether wisdom is learned or if it is a natural gift, everyone doesn't have it! Let's be clear!

What do you have that you thought your parents/caregivers should have had but they didn't? Write it out!

Listen, please stop trying to get someone to see their wrongs, get them to apologize or feel remorseful, or try to get them to sincerely love you. It wastes your time! I know you probably don't want to hear this. However, I extend my empathy, sympathy, and compassion to you and your life. Some of you reading this book have gone through things I cannot imagine! If I could imagine it, it would bring me to tears.

The best thing you can do is to focus on yourself! Not on what you missed out on or what you didn't get or should have gotten. God spoke this to me one day, "Shema, you are putting your parents in my place… your parents were not called to heal you, your parents were not called to make you whole, your parents were not called to reveal the pathway of your destiny, which I have created for you! Please stop putting my responsibilities on your parents." Wow, is that a showstopper? My parents are not my all answering God! For that, I had to repent, i.e., change my mind and viewpoint.

Our parents have to depend upon God for their healing and corrections, just like we do. No one is exempt! We are all called to look at God and not at each other. As you seek to come to know God more and read his word (bible) more, you will see your thoughts and habits begin to change. Answers will come, and you will start to feel better, understand better, build confidence, and more!

When I started drawing closer to him and reading more, not only did my life change, but my life also changed for my children! Everything I was missing "upstairs   " came to me through the bible. I KID YOU NOT! How to view people, control my emotions, not get my way, discipline, honor, respect, protection, patience, longsuffering, loyalty, success, finances, healing, and pain. How to speak and how to live.

People thought it was some secret counseling or education, but nope, it was simply me getting to know God in a real way! I now had a brain and solid information to guide my conversations and intelligence! Talk about unstoppable confidence!

I began hearing comments from others, such as: You have the secret blueprint to success. How did you get your kids like that? Or have you changed for the better? I'm proud of you. Can we keep in touch? I just want to be a part of your life; you bring life to me.

These are true comments and testimonies. These are only a few, but there have been so many more! Most of these people have no clue who I was or how I used to be! Family is not always the best way to get validation; they only see you as a child or someone who remembers you. Most family members are either not saved, religious, claim to be saved but do not walk in spiritual places, or live a life of mediocrity. These compliments come from co-workers and strangers (judges, state troopers, nurses, dancers, artists, doctors). I never would have thought I would be connected to people like them!

Why?

#1. I'm that stupid, unloved, neglected, smelly-haired, robbing, stealing, mean, fighting, no brain having, thugged out, living in the projects, section eight with one kid looking', no clothes matching, food stamp collecting, no college education, getting facade, and wealthy family looking girl!

That girl found one truth! I had one aunt who shared the Spirit of the bible with me, not only in word but in lifestyle as well! That girl took one thought and applied it with the thought of "What if this is true?" My aunt put actions behind her words, which led to me trusting her, which helped me to follow the truth and know that it was the truth!

The truth of the bible turned me from girl #1 into girl #2. I'm that highly intellectual, self-motivated, gorgeous, self-loved, creative, entrepreneurial boss! Educated, humble, God-anointed, financially independent, funny, the mother of the century, and a thought-provoking leader! The healed, whole, and helpful girl that doesn't take sh__! That girl!!

Truth: When you look at the difference between my girl#1 and girl #2, it seems like it probably took a long time to get there and a lot of help! The journey is not as tedious as it may sound. Remember, you are not alone! God is real and will do much of the work in you. It is not you who does it. Take one step, and he will take two. God will guide you to the right person, the right place, and the right information!
Your job is to say, "Yes, Lord"! Listen and be obedient to his word, open to receiving what he has for you in your heart, and apply it!!

Now, back to eras, lol... What era are you in? What's hot in society now? Equal rights for all, an era of LGBTQ+ (era of decreased number of children being born) due to man on man, woman on woman, men discarding their natural reproductive organs as well as women to become another sex or no sex at all. This is an era of confusion, disdain for heterosexuals, and pushed agendas!

This era is focused on sexuality and physical safety for all (human trafficking, molestation/abuse, pornography, neglect, the elderly and disabled), the right to be whatever you want to be, silencing and governing religion in public sectors, technology/virtual progression, drastic economic changes, closing racial disparities, greater capitalism than any era before, changes in food supplies and animals (cloning, stem cells), drastic climate changes with increased natural disasters, the era of space travel for civilians, the era of no commitment (fewer people believe in marriage), and a few more historical movements as well. Many of these are intended to lead society away from God, righteousness, peace, love, and the will of our creator!

After reading the last paragraph, what kind of things or mistreatment will come out of this era of parenting? Unfortunately, you are not the last person to go through this; more are coming behind you. Every era brings a different set of problems #truth# Please consider how the pendulum has swung! 1. In two eras, it was okay to beat and marry or abuse women and children. Sometimes, the woman is the abuser, I understand! In my era, it was less ok. In your era, it is not okay at all!

Meaning: we are progressing as a people and society! In your era, people do not want to work or take very little pride in customer service or quality. In schools and other facilities, not only can you not hit a kid, but you can't hug them either! You can barely even touch a kid because the abuse and neglect are so bad. Some kids also cry wolf when they know it isn't true. Physical touch is being demolished.

I had a cousin who did that once (cried wolf), but thankfully, she came clean, and everything was okay. However, when a generation of kids does not receive the correct discipline, love, or guidance, the atmosphere has changed to (do and be whatever feels right to you) with no more prayer or bibles in schools: just figure it out as you go! Sad devastation is waiting to happen in our North American nation!

Many parents/caregivers are afraid to say anything or touch a kid because now it can be taken as inappropriate. In return, the child inherits more conflicting emotions and thoughts. These equals decreased guidance, detachment during conversations, a lack of disciplinary action, less support, frustration, confusion, false empowerment, a lack of love, loneliness, and ultimately depression.

There are always pros and cons to each situation! What struggles are to come in your era? What can you do to make it easier or better for those who are about to experience trauma or are going through it right now? You will meet others, and when you do... what do you have to offer that will help change their life?

Truth: Some people should not have children!

Truth: No one is perfect.

Truth: You can change your situation!

Truth: Everyone does not know how to discipline children in a healthy way or out of love.

Truth: Everyone does not have your specific gifts, talents, or skills. Only God can show you how he wants you to use your pain with your gifts to bring about change for your community, the world, and His kingdom! God sees when no one else hears you or sees you, or recognizes your value, skills, talents, or possibilities! He knows! Trust him! He is the truth and the life!

As you complete the worksheets at the end of this chapter, you will feel some freedom of thought begin to take place and a shift in your mindset. This is the beginning of releasing lies and gaining clarity for yourself!

> **Listen to track: Don't wanna Stop (album I Am)**

Chapter 5
Worksheet

Before starting these worksheets, it is required that you write every answer down! Do Not think of the answers only! Please write below each question!

1. What signs were you looking for in childhood and maybe today?
Ex: love, trust, loyalty, dependability, truth, etc.

2. Are you still trying to change someone? Yes or no? Is it the person who offended you?

If yes, why? Is it working? Yes or no? Let's start by taking steps to stop AND let it go! You can only control yourself! If not, you are on the right track!

3. What era are you currently growing up in?

4. What era did your parents grow up in?

5. Were you able to empathize with others? Yes, or no? If not, why not? Write below!

As you adjust your mind and habits, return to this page and write down the comments you are getting from others about your changes!
Ex: I'm proud of you, you did good, I love you, you look great, you've changed, etc.

6. Describe the person you are/were.

7. Describe the person you would like to become!

8. List four truths out of this chapter that resonated with you!

1.
2.
3.
4.

Chapter 6
Who Told You To?

Who told you to hit me? Who told you I said that? Who told you I did that? Who told you to leave me? Abused, neglected, abandoned.... again, ugh. I find it funny (actually, I don't) how parents/caretakers who are neglectful or abusive or have even abandoned you... somehow believe that they know you!

This, too, caused me confusion mentally. Maybe you can relate? I often knew exactly how I felt, thought, and intentions. However, sometimes I would encounter an adult, and they would say, "You're lying!" I would think, "Who told you that?" One of my grandmother's church friends stayed over for a few weeks; Grandma was gone, and I was watching TV. I decided to go to the restroom. While washing my hands, I looked down; a $1 bill was on the floor! Of course, I was happy, lol!! I was around seven or eight years old. I ran and told Grandma's friend. She frowned, looked at me, and asked in a scowling voice, "Where did you get that dollar?" I said hesitantly, "I got it in the bathroom off the floor."

She looked at me with that scowling face and said, "You're lying. You took it out of my purse!" My first thought was, "Didn't she hear me?" This conversation was repeated four more times! She was so mean and sure that I did it. I began to think maybe I had lied and didn't know I had done it. What is a lie? How did I lie? Who told you that? Maybe it was Mom; she says I lie. She told my grandma I had lied and stolen from her purse! Finally, she made me go to my room and told me to stay there.

When Grandma got home, I ran out and told her what had happened! Grandma didn't seem bothered, as if she didn't believe what her friend had said. That made me feel so good, protected and heard. I felt I could trust my grandma! Now, whether she was trying to make me feel all of that or not, I don't know, but she did! She probably never knew what that meant to me! Grandma's friend may have had other motives; I'm not sure. What I do know is that perpetrators will often do something similar.

Take your pure thoughts and intentions and convince yourself that you asked for something you didn't or you like something when you know you don't! They are so confident that it causes you to question, well, maybe I do like it and don't know that I do. Maybe I did ask for it but didn't know that I did. It's very confusing and manipulative. It leaves an open door to destroy a person mentally, emotionally, financially, and physically. This is another form of abuse.

I have seen this tactic used in sex trafficking. I have seen older people get sucked into bad situations with this strategy of confusion. If adults fall for it, what chance does a child have?

So far, I hope you are enjoying my personal stories because sharing my embarrassments is not easy! Plus, I took a big step to go against the grain. Again, like many families, I'm sure some in my family who may read this book will think, "Why does she air her business out like that?" Or it's private, and what goes on in the house stays in the house. Well, I say to you that I never understood how adults are so much more willing to protect adults over kids. I've never agreed with that strategy if I've been able to comprehend it.

I tell my life story to help those going through what I went through as a kid. There was no YouTube, TikTok, IG, Twitter, Snapchat, Facebook, or anyone to talk to or guide me on handling the dysfunction. It gave me a bad start in life. I wish someone would have loved me enough to protect me, tell me, show me, help me, see me, encourage me, and take care of me mentally, emotionally, spiritually, financially, and physically until I could properly do it on my own.

Now, I can offer that to someone else! All the praise and acknowledgment go to God, my true father!!! From birth to seventeen, I had to deal with neglect even though my parents were not able to see it. The hardest part was the information or lies my parents would receive about me. My mother based her knowledge of me on my father! She viewed me as a liar and a spy. I have his tendencies, and he left me in that box! On the other hand, my father didn't really know me. Sometimes, he would get my character mixed up with my sister's.

Example: One night, my best friend, Brittle, wanted to hang out with her boyfriend, so she asked me to hang out with them. So, we devised a story to tell Dad so he would let me go. The story was that it was her birthday and would be at Circus Circus. Can I go? The answer was hesitantly, yes. We took the bus to meet her boyfriend. I knew he was from the Piru set (Blood). He had a friend I went to school with named D. So, we walked to the store, got some snacks, and went to his sister's house. His sister was putting her kids to sleep, so we entered her boyfriend's room.

We chilled for a while; then D decided to go to the store, and he left. Some other guy came into the room. He was trying to get at me, but I wasn't interested; plus, I was good chilling with D. About thirty minutes later, suddenly, the guy jumped up and ran out of the house!

My best friend and her boyfriend just looked at each other, confused. "What's wrong with him?" Next, about ten to twelve females came in the room, accusing me of sleeping with that guy! The next thing I know, I'm fighting twelve bitches from Donna Street Crips! My so-called "best friend" is petrified! She isn't moving at all! She is stuck in fear, shock, or something! I'm yelling at her, "Bitch get up and fight!" Her boyfriend, a BLOOD, answered the call and helped me fight!

(Side note: I hung more with Crips and GPKs aka Gerson Park Kings, not Bloods. They broke chairs over his back, and at one point, they pulled out a butcher's knife, trying to cut me and my clothes off; I had cuts and gashes on my legs. At least I had a Nike footprint on my face that was there for a good year! I guess his sister called the police because they came and broke it up.)

We made it back to Brittle's house; her big sister started laying hands on her when we walked through the door. I sat waiting for my father. When he walked through the door, he didn't say anything. He just started swinging his belt and knocked me out of the chair and then some! As he yelled at me, "You better not get pregnant! You at the hotel with a bunch of niggas?" I thought (who told you that?) When we got home, he beat me more, but instead of a belt, he switched to an extension cord without asking, listening, or being concerned – nothing! He quickly believed the misinformation given to him. That was one of the worst nights of my life! For that night's worth of beatings, I know I jumped into Criphood and Bloodhood, No doubt!

One thing was for sure! From there on out, E and I from Piru had an everlasting bond, and the "best friend" she kept hid from me. She already knew what the code was for punkin' out!

Blood was oozing from everywhere. How was I going to sleep tonight?
   I remembered Mom had bought me some silk pj's just a month ago. I tried them on! When I woke up the next morning, my silk pajamas were stuck to my skin! All the cuts, lacerations, and bleeding from butcher knives and extension cords had dried up and stuck to them. I slowly and gently tried to peel them off of my body so I could put on school clothes. I'd rather go to school than stay another minute in that house!

My pj's weren't coming off. They were peeling my scabs off as I attempted to remove them.   Let's try water, I thought. Maybe if it is wet enough, they will come loose.   I finally changed into my clothes. I went to school and thought I could have been killed last night, and my parents don't even know! They have never talked to me or listened to me. They don't know me; they believe what others say and never ask about me or what I experience or go through.

I am fifteen or sixteen; it still is unclear what love is. What is trust? What is truth? I just don't think this is love. There is nothing here for me; finding someone who can help, tell, or maybe show me is best. I spent an entire year with a shoe print on my face, and no one questioned it, at least not my parents. I don't think they looked in my face often enough to notice.

So, I made it to school. With pain, frustration, and more emotions pent up. However, I found someone I thought I could trust: my home economics teacher. She was always nice, never criticized me, and was open to listening to all her students! She seemed to be compassionate. She told me to talk to a school counselor. The next thing I knew, me and my sister were at CPS, Child Haven, in Las Vegas. I'm unsure how long I was there: maybe two to three weeks. As I sat there, I wondered why no one came for me, but at the same time, I kind of didn't expect it.

Maybe while I'm here, I thought I might find true love/compassion, someone who could make things clear and give me a better life. Well, that didn't happen. The staff had attitudes: some were mean, and some were okay. No one ever said anything positive or good about me. They were just there to work, and no one saw me. I didn't get to see my sister, either. I wondered if she was okay – if they were treating her well. I knew my best friend, Icy, knew where I was. She had been at school with me before I saw the counselor.

Somehow, my mother came and picked me up. She notified me that Dad never told her I was missing or at Child Haven. I guess he didn't want to lose custody and have to pay child support.

Many parents/caregivers do not know their children. Had my father known me – how I think, my character, and my soul – the moment someone said, "Shema, hotel, full of boys," he would have automatically known it was a lie or something wasn't right with the story. "I would maybe believe that with my other daughter, but not Shema."

How many situations have you had where lies or manipulation were used against you, and no one believed you or even asked you? I know it hurts and makes you feel lonely and unprotected. The more I talked to my friends at school and watched people in my family, the more I realized that most people operate on a system called lies or games!

You can call it fronting, faking, plastic, uncertainty, or hiding. I have been learning about neglect and abuse all my life. I can spot a person who is broken very easily. I can frequently tell when people are a front or lie because of intimidation, embarrassment, or manipulation. Nothing is worse than not being heard or understood when you need help!! Especially when those closest to you are not listening.

I came to the point where I realized that strangers and friends were quicker to help me than my own family. Is this correct? It doesn't sound correct... doesn't sound like love, doesn't sound like support. How can a stranger show more compassion than your own family? I still haven't figured that out! (actually, I have, but we'll skip that explanation) I concluded that it definitely is a heart issue!

Definitions

Neglect: failure to care for properly.
Abuse: treat (a person or an animal) with cruelty or violence, especially regularly or repeatedly (mentally, spiritually, physically, emotionally).
Exploitation: the action or fact of treating someone unfairly to benefit from their work (money, resources).

As you read the definitions above, understand that all three are different forms. Abuse can be physical (punching, slapping, spitting on), emotional (offering safety, then taking it away or saying they love you but treating you like they hate you), mental abuse (lies, manipulation, control), spiritual (forcing you to pray to devils or participate in demonic practices such as drinking blood or torturing others, witchcraft),

Neglect can be not providing food or shelter, not caring for you when you are sick, such as giving medicine or hospital care, not listening, or being attentive to your cries for help.

Exploitation can be using your disability check to go shopping for themselves, eating the food that you purchased without your permission, or denying you access to your property so that they can have it or use it.

For example, human trafficking is not only abuse; it is neglect and exploitation. The victim works, and the offender keeps all the profit with little to zero health care for the victims.

As in the previous chapter, Mom never saw her check the thirteen years my parents had been together. Mom worked, and Dad kept all the money; when they divorced, Mom got nothing (= abused, neglected, and exploited)!

As you are reading this book, please understand that I might be healed, but I still have scars! I wear them daily, unfortunately. I have both physical scars from fights and beatings, emotional scars from neglect, and mental scars from watching my mom be abused. Sometimes, they can be tender, but for the most part, they do not cause pain anymore.

I have learned how to handle people and families who still operate off the old systems. In the beginning, you will need to avoid them because they don't know any better, and many times, they will try to convince you it's right.

The majority of the time, they will not be able to hear you when you try to change their view give them the correct way, or share what God has shown you, especially if they are older than you and live in religion. It's like speaking to what Christians call "Pharisees or Sadducees"; they miss the moves of God because they have him in a box.

God will show you who to distance yourself from, what to speak, when, and how to deliver the message. He will also tell you when and if you are to return to your family. Just know that you will be talked about, and everyone will not understand the new you! They did not understand Jesus's ways; if he is who you chose to follow and listen to, they won't understand it, either. Only those who truly walk in the spirit realm will know and understand his ways and you! Stay close to your heavenly father and be obedient, regardless of what anyone says or thinks!

Take your time working on the worksheets at the end of this chapter. It may bring some tears to your eyes. Many times. We have never put a name to what we have gone through. As you go through these exercises, DO NOT hold your tears back! If you have a private space to do this in, take it. Crying and feeling hurt, pain, and disappointment is a way to accept the truth and cleanse your soul and your mind!

It is not comfortable rehashing the past, but if you don't, it will be extremely difficult to heal properly and get past it.

Remember! YOU ARE NOT ALONE... God is with you through this process, and he will do work in you that you cannot do in yourself! Take one step, and God will take two. The entire reason why I am writing this book is because God led me to. I NEVER had plans to write a book for teens/young adults/adults. Once God places something in your heart, it's impossible not to do it! This book is for you, the one who is reading this book and crying or getting upset... you who have been trying to find answers. YOU! God knows, and he sees you, and he hears you! He saw every single tear! Every single offense! Keep reading this book, as there is more to come! Jesus loves you truly!!!

> **Try worship music from my new album, I Am, as you work on these worksheets!**

Chapter 6
Worksheet

Before starting these worksheets, it is required that you write every answer down! Do Not think of the answers only! Please write below each question!

1. What kind of scars are you wearing?
Ex: physical, emotional, mental, spiritual, etc.

2. What cup of vinegar did you grow up in?
Ex: abuse, neglect, abandonment, etc.

3. What are 1 or 2 things that make you choke up or cry whenever you think about it?

We must dig deeper into these things to heal you and move forward in peace.

4. Are you alone in this process?

If not, you're doing good! If yes, continue reading the chapters; you still haven't gotten It yet. Just marinate on it! (selah)

5. Can you name one person who truly loves you? Write your answer and their name below.

Chapter 7
Trust Who?

You quickly learn who you can trust and who you cannot! There have been times when I wondered, "What price will I pay if I trust this new person?" Will they hurt me? Embarrass me?

How can you tell if you can trust someone? I was taught growing up that if you need help, get an adult! Unfortunately, many of us had that trust broken. Instead of running to adults, we ran away from them. I cannot tell you how many times I ran away from home. I have lost count! The place that was supposed to be a nurturing, safe space for me – a place to learn, grow, and develop – what happened to it?

What happened to the families I saw on TV? Some of my friends had it! How did they get it? Why didn't I have it? What did they know that I didn't? I guess my parents don't know it either or surely life would be better, like the Huxtables!
One adult after another failed me. Trust who?

As I returned to my mother's house from CPS and school, I looked forward to seeing my friend, Icy. We would ditch school together and have boyfriends and double dates, although we never met each other's families. She was one friend I could talk to honestly without being too embarrassed! Unfortunately, it ended abruptly when an unexpected twist happened! My mother had a new boyfriend. I didn't like him, but Mom didn't seem to care how I felt, anyway.

He began taunting me. He would say, "My daughter goes to your school, but I can't tell you who she is." Then he starts telling lies to my mother! So immature, I thought. Not again! Another adult who is extremely aggravating and lies to kids! Again, I tell Mom, but she doesn't believe me. I'm used to it now, but... damn! She took a strange man's word over mine. She took a strange man over me!

You know how besties are! "Icy, let's find out who this girl is so she can come get her daddy!" We never found her. Then, Icy and I received a class assignment to bring a picture of our families to school. Hmmmmm, when we got to school the next day, we traded photos. As I looked at Icy's photo, my mouth fell open in disbelief! Icy! This is the man, this is him!" She said, "Who is who?" This is the man at my house all the time. This is the man that I told you about! She responded, "No, that's my dad."

"What? What?" I said. "That's the man that be at my house."

She responded, "No, that's my dad!" We repeated that conversation three more times before she was so upset that she snatched the photo and walked out of the classroom. Icy quit being my friend. I was both hurt, upset, and betrayed all at the same time! Trust who?

Yes, Mom and I argued numerous times about the situation. Finally, after being called a bitch and being invited outside to fight her, I left it alone and realized once again that I was not important. It really is all about adults and what they want! My thoughts are of no value, my life is of no concern, and my need for guidance and trust is not on anyone's list. Embarrassing! It is clear now: I don't get love. It is only for certain people.

Mom's boyfriend told Lie number one: Shema used your social security number, called the phone company, changed the phone plan, and increased the bill. I watched this stranger lie to my grandma, aunts, and his wife and family. What a creep! There is more, but for the sake of being modest, I won't include the worst parts of this story.

What teenager do you know who worries about bills and house phone plans?
While my sister and I starved for love, attention, guidance, and more, the adults were in their own world. Eventually, my sister got tired of his lies and aggravation! So, she took her shoe off and threw it at Mom's boyfriend, hitting him in the back of the head ! He called my sister a bitch, then left and went home (as he should have). However, my sister was younger than me. I'm sure the lack of protection and love, and

again watching Mom accept this strange man over her and me, really impacted her life in the wrong direction. Again, trust who? No one listens.

If you have been neglected, abused, or exploited, I'm sure you are familiar with these experiences. You may be in that very situation right now! If you are, do the worksheets at the end of this chapter! There are great steps to help you develop a plan to protect yourself and how to find someone you can trust.

Hear me now! When you have been so used to being lied to and are extremely familiar with it. Whether you know it or not, you begin to attract those kinds of people without knowing it. It doesn't have to just be lies. It can be manipulation/manipulative people, abuse/abusive people, and/or control/controlling people.

I ended up having children with a manipulative/lying person; then, I ended up marrying a habitual bold-faced liar. So, how do you break this cycle and ensure your future doesn't have these consistent hiccups?

I guarantee that it will be too late to realize what you have done to yourself if you do not complete these worksheets and get your mind right! We can say all day long, "I'm never going to be like..." The truth is that 90% of the time, you end up with the same habits as the offender, or you get into a relationship with someone just like that but in a different form. As for me, I was mean as hell, demeaning, manipulative, inconsiderate, bossy, ungrateful, selfish, and more, but one thing I'm not... is a liar!

At one point, my five-year-old son yelled at me, "You're just a mean old lady"! (I was twenty-four.) That was one of my wake-up moments! Unlike my parents/caregivers, I did love my son to the point where I was willing to readjust to ensure he was a happy kid who loved being at home. I HEARD HIM!

Sometimes, you may feel as if you can't even trust yourself! Have you ever felt that way? Maybe you can't trust yourself to make the right choices, or you can't trust your judgment of character and people. This is understandable when you have never seen honesty and may not be sure what it truly means. You may not trust your judgment when no one has taught you how to think or view circumstances.

Maybe adults have broken your trust so many times that trust no longer exists in your vocabulary. Trust who? So confusing... hmm.... I know. There are two people you must learn to trust if you want to make it out of these situations and have a renewed mindset and a successful future!

#1. You
#2. God

By the time you have completed this book, you should have a different point of view, a plan to get unstuck and move forward, a sense of relief, some healing, and the courage to do this and that this is not all that life has for you!

This is not the end. There is more: there is better! You don't have to see how or when. Just trust that God has a bright future for you, one you could have never imagined!! You are not reading this book for nothing! Jesus had me write this book just for people like (me) I used to be, for people like you!

You will also find steps on what to do about your offender and the offenses. The entire point of this book is to set people free from oppression, depression, and suicidal ideation. To get you to a place where you do not feel unloved and alone but are confident and happy. The love will definitely come in two or three ways.

#1. You will receive an unexplainable love from God; this is a better experience than an explanation!

#2 You will comprehend and experience what it is like to love yourself!

#3. Others around you will begin to show you different forms of love (not sexual): co-workers, neighbors, partner.

It will be difficult to recognize or receive love without going through a healing process, changing your mindset, and learning to trust yourself and God again.

What is love?

Google's definition: 1. an intense feeling of deep affection. "Babies fill parents with feelings of love." 2. a great interest and pleasure in something. "His love for football."

I disagree with these definitions. They could end up meaning "his love for violating young boys" or her love for beating on kids. Maybe that is an internal love of passion, but it is not an outward expression of love toward another. The TRUE definition of love is John 3:16. God loved the world so much that he sacrificed his son to save us all!

Ephesians 5:25-33: Husbands love your wife as Christ loved the church and died for it.

LOVE IS SACRIFICE!!! It is a sacrificial choice motivated by a feeling or thought that moves you to action. (Shema Ladd)

Example: I'm hungry, but I'll give my last to the kids instead of eating.

Example: Instead of ignoring what's happening, let me step up and stand up to protect and guide. Or I may have to take sexual/physical abuse for my child to protect them.

Example: Instead of being with this woman/ man, meth house, let me die to what I want and choose my family

Example: Instead of manipulating/lying to them, let me accept responsibility and take the hit for my choices.

Example: I Don't have time, but let me listen and advise my children. I will just have to be late for work or my date.

Example: I have a trip to go on. I know my aunt likes to make the kids drink their urine, but they will be ok this time... wait! No, I will cancel to protect my kids and break the cycle!

Example: I will go to counseling even though I don't want anyone to know my secrets. I will get help.

Love ensures your sacrifice will leave the other person in a better position than before! I do not believe I need to explain what love is not! It sounds simple, but Jesus did not want to die! Like most adults don't want to die either.

In Matthew 26:39, Jesus prayed, "Father, if it is possible let this cup pass from me." He did not want that pain! Yet, Jesus was far stronger and disciplined than our caretakers/parents. He saw what the result would be for our future if he went through with it! He suffered so that we do not have to anymore.

Some of you reading this book may have gone through very similar abuse as Jesus did. By Jesus simply voicing his Identity and declaring what his mission was, others became angry, offended, scoffers, jealous, and intimidated. Even if Jesus lied, was that reason good enough to kill him? A "friend" set him up, a mob took him, beat him, whooped him, tore his skin, spit on him, put a crown of sharp thorns on his head, stuck a spear in his side, nails through his hands and feet pinned to a wooden cross with blood everywhere!

How much more painful is that? Was it that serious? The city watched it, and no one stood up to help him. Someone says, "Lonely and humiliating"! Trust who? It is the knowledge that will set you free!

Read your bible even if you can't comprehend it, pray daily, and watch what happens! Whether your offense came from foster care providers, adoptive parents, CPS, APS, school teachers, staff, family members, neighbors, police officers, church pastors, staff, or Boy Scout leaders, I have heard and seen it all! Even with broken trust and confusion, your life can be different!

It is true! You are loved even if you don't feel it! God sees you; he is listening! You can trust him! You may be asking, "If I can trust him, where was he when?" I felt the same way at one point, but he did show up and explain it all to me. He did have a purpose and a plan for my life! I had to understand first that HE IS GOD! He doesn't think like us; his ways are bigger than ours. (Isaiah 55:8-9).

He sees the beginning and the end, while we only see glimpses and pieces! You WILL be able to trust again; you may not see it right now, but you will!
If you don't trust anyone or anything else...

TRUST THIS BOOK! TRUST ME!

Listen to the track: Smile Again (album Who Am I)

Chapter 7
Worksheet

Before starting these worksheets, it is required that you write every answer down! Do Not think of the answers only! Please write below each question!

1. Who is in your life now that you can trust?

2. Name four ways in which someone has broken trust with you.

   1.
   2.
   3.
   4.

3. What did you trust them with?
Ex: Your emotions? Your mind? Your heart? Your purity? Your life? Your children? You?

4. How do you handle the unexpected?

5. How do you handle disappointments?

6. What are your reactions to these situations usually?

Steps to locating a trustworthy person:

A. Research their online presence, social media, Google, etc., and what they post about. What clues do you see that may be warning signs?

B. What is their reputation? Does what they do in private match how people view them in public? If not, that's a warning sign!

C. What kind of "vibes" do you get from that person? Trust your gut feeling!

D. Are they a good listener, or do they talk more than they listen? (You want a listener!)

E. Do they rush you? Do you feel hurried when speaking with them? (this is not the right person)

F. Are they a giver or a taker? Do they add to your life or subtract from it? (you want an adder!)

G. Are they overly touchy? Rubbing your arms or back too long and close yet listening so intently? (Warning sign!)

Pray and ask God for discernment as you look for someone trustworthy. The definition of discernment is to be able to judge well! These are just a few ways to identify a trustworthy person.

7. Do you trust yourself? Yes or no? If not, list the reasons below.

Trusting yourself can be learned!

YOU WILL BE BETTER AT IT ONCE YOU COMPLETE THIS BOOK AND WORKSHEET EXERCISES. This is a foundational building book!

Here are some steps to get rid of your (sexual AND physical abuse) offender! As scary as it may seem, you must take action yourself. If you are at school, tell a trustworthy staff member. If no one is trustworthy, figure out how to use a phone to call an abuse hotline or 9-1-1. They will temporarily remove you from the home, and the offender will be removed and hopefully charged AND jailed! When speaking to someone, be clear that you never want to see that person again (if that's how you truly feel).

Each circumstance is different, but you must avoid the perpetrator if you want safety. I have seen where the perpetrator is removed and returned because Mom or Dad allowed it. You must be clear and vocal to whoever comes to help you!

I know that sometimes grief, pain, confusion, lack of seeing an end, or a happy future can be overwhelming! It can make you question, "Why am I here?" Let me tell you now! Suicide is not the answer! I get it! But there is more!

Take these steps to get over the trauma and to the bright, sunny side. There is a sunny side!

8. Do you love yourself? Yes or no? Write below why or why not.

9. Write below 3 examples where you know God was with or protected you. Even during your traumatic experiences?

10. What is your love language? Circle one below!

   A. Acts of service (when people do things for you)

   B. Words of affirmation (you did well, you look good)

   C. Gifts

   D. Physical touch (cuddle, rubbing, etc.)

   E. Quality time (everyone is different)

Chapter 8
Who Am I?

The most important thing you can do for yourself is find out and know your true Identity! Do you know who you are? Do you know who you want to be? Do you know why and who God created you to be? You will have some clues and steps to discover by this chapter's end! #clarity!

So many things can easily and quickly rob you of your self-identity without knowing it! Usually, people do not realize they are lost until their memory is wiped out, they are extremely confused, they are so stressed that they can no longer function, and/or their lives are miserable. I can tell you for sure! I struggled with identity for most of my life! I do not want that to be your story.

The sooner you know who you are, the more confidence and focus you will have, the better your decision-making, and the clearer your direction in life will be! This means it will be more difficult for people to use, exploit, or manipulate you! Sounds good, right?

Let me tell you my stories, lol. As I told you in previous chapters, in the beginning, I was taught not to be like or look like Mom. That part was clear, and I knew I didn't want to be a girl! Around age three to four, Mama convinced Daddy to let us go to Texas to visit family – after many discussions and arguing, of course! Yay!

We get to go to Texas! So, we went to Texas to a house with people I do not know. There were three kids around my age: four, five, six... So, we all went to the back room to play, like most kids do! This story took a strange turn, though.

The other kids wanted to go to the bathroom but didn't need to, so I said no. After they asked me multiple times to go with them, I stood up and went to the bathroom. Suddenly, they closed the door, all standing together, looking at me! Then a strange question came: what color are you? "I'm yellow," I replied. They stared at me as If I had done something wrong. This feeling overcame me, and I only got it with my parents. I stood there, sort of afraid because I thought I was in trouble. Then they asked me to take my clothes off. "No," I replied.

They asked me this several times. Feeling like I did something wrong, I finally took my clothes off. Then, finally, Mom comes into the bathroom. There I was, the only kid standing with no clothes on! I thought for sure now I was really in trouble! None of the other kids had taken their clothes off, but they were all dark-skinned. For years, I wondered why they had me do that so they could stare at me.

When I started school, kids always asked me, "What color are you?" Finally, I asked Mom. She said, "Black," of course. I had to correct her, lol. "No, Mom, I'm yellow. I did not get the picture quite yet, lol.

On the next occurrence, Dad and I visited my Uncle Tony. While Dad and Uncle Tony were in the house talking, I decided to go outside and find some kids to play with. There was only one kid: this little girl on the other side of the silver-linked chain fence. I started talking to her, and she just stared quietly. Then she asked me, "What color are you?" I told her, "I'm black."

She looked at me and said, "No, you're not." We argued about that the whole time and never got to play together! This went on for years! Then the terminology was upgraded to "Are you mulatto?" I would just say no because I didn't know what that meant! Whatever it was, that wasn't me   .

It was between dealing with me not knowing who I was and other people not knowing what I was. Dark-skinned girls were picking on me; no one was talking to me or guiding me. I was an open canvas for anyone to tell me who I was or who they thought I should be. I learned to be whatever someone wanted me to be so we could get along and maybe have some fun. This was not a good thing! You see, this also included men and relationships. Thus, it was the beginning of my criminal activities!

I became more accustomed to hearing the term "trophy," as in "you're my trophy." Hmmm , what does that mean? I found out years later, unfortunately. I was left with thoughts like what's right and what's wrong. Where do I fit in? If it's not my color, it's my behavior or something else. Who am I? I will just find where I fit in and who will accept me as I am! Neglected, rejected, unprotected, and confused, I began connecting with other kids who had little to no supervision. Survival was the name of the game!

Dear reader, does any of this sound familiar to you? What group of peers did you fall into after your abuse/neglect, etc.? If you haven't made it that far, please read this chapter and Chapter 9! Complete the worksheets at the end of each of these chapters! It amazes me how I lived in the biggest city known for prostitution and sexual immorality (Las Vegas, NV), aka "Sin City," and I was never snatched! Human trafficking is one of the fastest-growing crimes and a multi-billion-dollar industry. Traffickers are always looking for neglected, rejected, and unprotected kids to profit from or "exploit." I am certain that I could have ended up as one of R. Kelly's victims or some other predator... talking about "keep it down low." lmbo .

The conditions were perfect! I ended up dating one of the hardest OG crips in Las Vegas and later had children with one of the biggest D-boys and pimps in town as well (in the nineties).   How did I end up with those two? I guess because I was a "trophy." Now I understand why I attract these kinds of men. My friends always told me my life was a storybook, but I thought it was normal. Lmbo. I am now trying to prevent these things from happening to you or someone you may know.

You may feel alone, unheard, unseen, unloved, and/or unprotected, but let's try to make decisions based on knowledge and not emotions! There are answers! I am talking to you right now if no one else is! Do you hear me? Are you listening? Social media is not the answer. There, you will only see what you WISH you were or wish you had. There, you will see people faking to get more viewers. You will see information you can't tell if it's true. Role models? How do you choose a good one?

Who do you think is a good role model for you? Please understand that just because someone is famous or has money does not mean they know who they are or are happy or safe! I have seen artists sing music that doesn't represent their true selves. They are miserable because now they are being controlled by someone else, and the music isn't true to their heart. They are being robbed. I have seen rich people beaten and abused by their partners because of jealousy. Money is not the answer. Finding your identity is the answer! Staying true to yourself is the answer!

Who told you who you were? Was it the mom who pulled your fingernails out? Was it the uncle, dad, cousin, and neighbor who molested and raped you daily? Or, for the guys, was it your female babysitter? Did they tell you that you are worthless? Just a piece of meat? A doormat, maybe? Was it the school teacher who said you were stupid, or your clothes were ugly? Was it your caretakers who told you that you were only a worker or slave? Who told you what you are? Maybe it was a boyfriend/girlfriend. What did they tell you?

Now, we have to rewrite the lies! The truth is the ONLY thing that can set you free! (John 8:32) What does God say about you? This is the only thing that matters! Jeremiah 29:11 says his thoughts are to do you good and give you a good future! 1 Peter 2:9 says he has called you out of darkness and into the light!

Zechariah 9:10 says he will deliver you out of the hand of your enemy.

In Genesis, God says he created us in his image! We are a peculiar people of royal priesthood. Most beloved of God. He also said not to prevent little ones from coming to him. It is better for a person to die than harm his children. This is the love of God and how he feels about you!

For many years, I looked at God as if he were just like my parents (mean, unconcerned, etc.). BOY was I wrong! Do not relate God to your offenders... he is nothing like that. 3 John 1:2 says that above all things, God's will is that you prosper in health, soul, and finances! This does not sound like abuse, or neglect was in his plan for us.

Another identity crisis I had was a lack of true femininity. My father was the dominant one, and I was not supposed to be like Mom. So, guess what? Through the years, many men have told me I act like a boy/man. Some liked it, while others did not. I was very controlling, mouthy, independent, strong, inconsiderate of feelings, hard, and aggressive. This made it hard to connect with other females who were feminine (gentle, forgiving, well-dressed, well-groomed, etc.). This left me either hanging with the guys or with girls who were thugging or gang-banging.

Abuse, neglect, and exploitation always lead to an identity crisis. Let me show you. Were you a boy who had uncles and cousins molesting you, beating you, dominating you? These are actions that most of society assumes men only due to women. If you are treated like a female (receiver), and that's your foundation, who taught you how to be a man (giver)? Where do you fit in at? Do you hang out with girls because you know how to act and be like one? Do you hang with the boys because your genetic makeup is male? The females may not accept you, and the males may not accept you either. So, now what? You find where you fit, right? Tired of being treated like a misfit or rejected, so you find your group of those accepted.

You may be gay, lesbian, transgender, or plus! What I can tell you is that If this has occurred through watching or experiencing abuse, neglect, or exploitation, that was never God's plan for your life! Romans 1:21-28 speaks of the perverse things that adults began to do that was an abomination and sin before God: man on man, woman on woman, spirits on mankind, etc. There is no judgment here: I grew up not wanting to be a girl and could have easily gone to the plus side! Lol.

For the sake of the time, we are currently in 2023. I must also mention that in keeping with spirits, getting involved is against God's commands. As I watched Demi Lovato speak on a TV show, she confessed, "I am Pan. I will receive love from anyone or anything," meaning (spirits and aliens). I sit and stare at the TV and listen to what she is saying. I think to myself, the bible speaks of these things. She doesn't profess to be a follower of Christ and apparently is not seeking to do so. Which the scripture doesn't apply to her. However, if you are forced or coerced into such activities, this would be considered spiritual abuse.

Example: I had a special needs client (Jay). A friend of his family wanted to pick him up for the weekend. I agreed although I had never met this person before. Long story short, the weekend turned into five days! When I contacted the family, they didn't know where their friend had taken Jay. Once we got Jay back, he began saying repetitive phrases and hateful words to me. Well, the family, his social worker, and I all knew something was terribly wrong. When I asked Jay what had happened, he said, "I didn't get any sleep. They kept me up the whole time, saying many words… chanting."

I realized they were performing demonic/witchcraft practices and attempting to brainwash Jay! Yes, spiritual abuse does exist! It took months to get his mind and spirit right, but with the right support, we did it! That attack was used on Jay but intended for me. You must have spiritual eyes and intelligence to understand what takes place. God's protection and the leading of the Holy Spirit led us to find Jay in a whole different city than where he lived. The Holy Spirit taught me what to pray and what to do to deliver Jay from what had happened to him.

Luckily, the secular and religious case managers and behavior specialists were supportive… only because they knew it was obvious that something had gone terribly wrong for Jay. They did not know what to do or want to touch spiritual things; they felt unqualified to do so.

Many of these situations are spiritual! How many times have you looked at a person and said, "Something is wrong with them," or she's mean, she's vulgar, and he is perverted? Have you ever watched the movie "Exorcist"? Where do you think they came up with such movies? Most people don't like to discuss it unless it's in the form of a movie or board game (i.e., a joija). Demonic spirits are real, and many people do not realize that they are being influenced or used by them every day.

Society prefers to talk about heaven and skip over hell or the devil. Others choose to believe that neither exists. Be careful and aware of what and who you are allowing to influence you (social media, celebrities, peers, coworkers, etc.). Where are they leading you? You'd better know for yourself!

If you desire to be as you were created, this journey will be a difficult one... but NOT Impossible! It is about your heart, willingness to obey, and prayer life. Finding your identity is a lot more than working through your offenses! As I grew up, I knew there were things I loved to do, whether it was natural or developed through neglect.

I loved to sing and dance! Unfortunately, no one in my house or family saw my talents; if they did, they didn't say anything. So, I went through my life being trained to work at a job! I went to school with a girl named Kameelah William. She was with the musical girls' group, "702".

We had the same guy friend, Broderick. After school, Broderick and I would talk on the phone; he liked to hear me sing. Then, he would talk to Kameelah and listen to her. When the news hit that she was in 702, and we heard her music playing on the radio station 88.1 KCEP, I was happy for her. Yet, at the same time, I was jealous. I wondered how she was able to do that. What kind of parents did she have? Why didn't my parents support me? Why couldn't they see that I could do things? I remember asking Mom, "Mama, didn't you say you used to love to dance?" She replied, "Yes".

I sat silently, pondering her answer. Then, I asked, "Why did you stop dancing?" She replied, "I don't know". Again, I sat pondering. I clearly remember saying to myself. "I don't know how that happened, but I love to dance and will never stop dancing. My body won't let me." We must have different definitions of "I love to dance." Lol.

Your family often will not see the gifts and talents you naturally hold. Even if they do, it doesn't mean they will help you, support you, or do anything about it. I was always selected as a soloist in everything I did! My teachers saw it, so why didn't my parents? In the 4th grade, I was a violinist, but couldn't read music. My violin teacher was so impressed with my violin skills that she really wanted me to stay in the class. She always wrote my notes differently for me (A, D, D, E, F.). I was the only violinist in class who received a solo part in our recitals!

I won my first talent show in the 5th grade for singing. In the 6th grade, my choir teacher gave me a solo in the Christmas performance. (Dad attended this one with my stepmom.) At church, the praise director gave me solos as we traveled from church to church, singing. The only time I really got to dance was on the west side of Las Vegas.

There was a cultural suite called the "Heritage" on Owens Street. On weekends, a lady was teaching African dance! I did everything I could to get into her class! Dancing brought life to my soul! My talents were completely ignored with no support. Who are you? What can you do?

Dear reader, who are you? By the time I reached high school, I was rapping and writing my lyrics, and no one could beat me at dancing! Yet again, I had gone so long without support and encouragement that I would shy away from some things.

Take the high school talent show! Some girls did fashion modeling. (I didn't have clothes for that.) Some did sing, rapping, and other things. My confidence was not available. They had parents in the audience to support and guide them. I was alone with no identity. So, I sat quietly, watched, and periodically laughed. On the inside, I was lost, confused, and hurt. I spent most of my time at Larry's Sight & Sound (a music store) on the west side by Grandma's house.

I loved music so much that my cousin, D. and I would write music together. Eventually, as I got older, I had to put it aside and get a job. Even now, as an adult, I get the same responses. "You sing so beautifully; you should do an album!"

My achievements:

Modeling school: a teacher wants me to run the class while she steps out.

Dance class: an instructor wants me to be at the front or enter competitions.

Karaoke: the crowd requests me to sing multiple songs, and the DJ always calls me to sing. These are gifts that have NEVER left my soul! When music comes on, my body moves without permission. Lol.

The worksheets at the end of this chapter will help you identify both seen and unseen gifts, talents, and passions. Find yourself! Find your identity! Your identity is not what happened to you! Make sure you do this even before you get into an intimate relationship!

As mentioned in a previous chapter, I married someone who did not suit me. This person belittled my singing voice and told me I couldn't sing. He embarrassed me in front of other dancers who aspired to be like me by insinuating that they should not dance like me. He also criticized how I raised my kids (not knowing how deeply rooted my love was for being a very active, present, supportive, and loving parent)
    Above all, he refused to read the bible with me (my core) He did all the wrong things just to control me!!! It was trauma all over again!

If you don't hear anything else from this book, hear this! Find your Identity from God's perspective! If your family doesn't truly know God, and they do not know you, they will never understand your decisions or guide you!

Who are you? What should your answer look like?

Example: Shema, who are you? I am a spiritual ambassador for the Kingdom of God, who was born into a dysfunctional family and made bad decisions. I am the daughter of a King (natural and spiritual), a creative, loving, healed, compassionate go-getter about developing businesses, programs, and resources to help others find their way and purpose. I am a mother, friend, protector, provider, confidant, and supporter of all who need guidance and trust. I am 25% Mafia (PTSD), 50% hood, and 25% Bougie! 100% true Christian!

Now, with that explanation, who do you think has the skills to manipulate me, lie to me, or convince me that I am a loser, trash, ugly, stupid, unlovable, bad parent, can't sing or dance, etcetera?

Answer: NO ONE!

I want you to get to that point! Remember that you are not alone! God wants you to know these things so you can fulfill your purpose!!!

> **Listen to the track: Who Am I (album Who Am I)**

Chapter 8
Worksheet

Before starting these worksheets, it is required that you write every answer down! Do Not think of the answers only! Please write below each question!

1. Is there a question multiple people always ask you? Yes, or no? What is that question?

For me, it was: "What color are you?" or "What are you?" If people ask you the same question repeatedly, they are trying to understand you.

2. Are you multi-racial and/or multicultural?

I am both!

On my father's side, I am "black and white". On my mother's side, I am "Indian and black," Although I appear to look more "black AND white." Most people cannot tell what I am (ambiguous)! I had to learn how to explain to others what I am and how to approach or interact with me.

I am also multi-cultural, meaning one side of my family is what many would call bougie or "uppity, maybe plastic! The other side of my family, some would call "urban" or "hood," is also down to earth, straightforward!

I had to learn that when I am around one side of my family, I should act and behave one way, and when I'm with the other side, I should behave differently! Why? Because neither side fully accepted the habits and behaviors of the other.

You, too, will find a balance to these issues!

3. How do people normally respond to you?

    A. Your smile?

    B. Your skin color?

    C. Your vibe?

    D. Your personality?

    E. Your talents/gifts?

These clues and tips will help you find your balance, acceptance, and inner-self validation! (Example on next page)

Example: Regardless of my color, I learned that one thing they all like is my smile! I also learned that my smile could get me a job. It will get me into the club, and it will get me a "yes" when someone wants to tell me no!

Example: I learned that because of my skin color, I can cross racial barriers and boundaries. How? Some people are not as offended or intimidated by my skin color, so they allowed me into their "club," and I learned what others could not. Now, that's not my problem; it's theirs! I just learned how to use what I got!

I also learned that some people did not like my skin color! Why? They knew I would get opportunities they would not get! Like the boy they really wanted, but he wanted me! Or the job they wanted, but the slightly racist manager chose me! You can't let others' insecurities or lack of understanding confuse or tell you who you are! They can't validate you! Only you and God can do that!

4. Whom are you trying to be like, but it doesn't fit you? Someone on TV? A friend? Another boy or girl? Write your answer below.

God made us all different, with different skills, talents, thoughts, etc. You can't be someone else!!! There is only one of them! Only ONE of you! Only ONE of me!

5. Do you make your decisions/choices based on how you feel? Or off knowledge? Holy Spirit lead?

6. If you have a role model, below, write a summary of what they stand for!
Ex: truth, integrity, honesty, helping others, drama, being a hater, cursing, beauty, etc.

When you are finished, take a long look at your list and make sure they are worthy to be your role model!

7. Write a list of all your gifts and talents below!
Ex: skateboarding, dancing, singing, surfing, coordinating events, tennis, etc.

8. What do people always tell you are good at?

9. What comes so easily to you that you think it is nothing?

10. What brings you joy every time you do it?

11. What makes you angry whenever you see or hear it?

12. Who are you?

Don't worry if your answer does not look so good. You are changing and who you now know yourself as, will change! Answer this question again in one year!

Chapter 9
Which Path Do I Take?

This is probably the most difficult chapter and worksheet you will work through. Recounting your offenses and offenders is the main step to receiving true healing. Forgiveness!

WHAT!! Forgive who??? They don't deserve forgiveness! They deserve to suffer a lifetime or die! I understand.

Vengeance is mine, says the Lord! (Romans 12:19). I went to church with a friend. She would tell me how, every night, her mother's boyfriend would come into her room and molest her. She explained how she told her mom, but her mom did not believe her. One day, she told me, "Shema, tonight, when he comes, I'm going to sleep with a butcher knife under my pillow, and I'm going to kill him." I thought, whoa, I guess she has no other option. I hadn't seen her for a few weeks after that. I was so nervous, and it was constantly on my mind.

When we met back up at church the next Sunday, she informed me that he never came home that night. The next morning, there was a knock at the door. The police were talking to her mom, and she tried to listen intensely. They notified her mom that her boyfriend had been in an accident with a semi-truck, and his head had been decapitated! Wow... now that's vengeance! A church service had a whole new meaning to me after that! I also saw God's love.... He didn't want blood on my friend's hands.

Another friend was violated by her father, yet she still has contact with him. He made it alive with his head intact! She had to learn many of the same things you are learning in this book, including forgiveness.

As for me, I have been inappropriately touched by family members but never raped nor molested by any of them, thank God . I even sit and listen as my sister tells me of family members who have touched her. Did I tell my parents? Yes, I informed my parents, and just like you and many others, nothing was done. Or maybe something was done, and I just didn't know about it! I didn't note one sign of anger, not one sign of defense, nor even a negative reaction in a facial expression. I guess they call these "family secrets".

How many family secrets have happened at your expense?

Regardless, it boils down to you and only you. So, what can you do? This is a hard pill to swallow, especially if you are still in that situation. Keep reading and use what you can until your situation changes. It WILL change! I do not want to give you the wrong idea, so let's clarify some things! Just because you walk through the healing process does not mean that you won't have scars or get hurt or disappointed again.

There are many emotions, and we will continue to experience most of them for the rest of our lives – including betrayal, backstabbing, jealousy, disappointment, anger, etc. The question is, what will you do with them?

I have even been recently betrayed while writing this book! My initial reaction to you ask.   Not gone lie! I have the hands to do it! And the people to do it for me! Someone says, "Reach out and touch somebody"   . My uncle is Peter, and my brother is Paul… okay, enough of that!!

Self-check: You must stop and hear what God is saying and his will! Aw   . Get silent. What did he show you?

Sometimes, the lesson is for you, while at other times, it is for the offender. Obedience is the best answer and keep your ears open. Even if you think obedience will make you look soft like a punk or a bust. It's not easy on either side of things, but obedience is your true answer. Your girl was obedient! I gave my best wishes and blessings and thanks for the times she was able to be a friend. Then I walked away from it!

Again, many won't understand your decisions or mode of reasoning, but standing in obedience and keeping your ear to God's will is more important than other's opinions or thoughts. Don't worry: if God wants to bring that relationship around again, you will know exactly why and your role in the situation!

Some people in your situation have simply "passed the buck," so to speak. Example: If two siblings grew up with alcoholic caregivers, they would usually do one of two things. One will become an alcoholic also, and the other will despise it and not drink at all or very seldom.

What was the addiction or problem that messed you and your siblings up? Drugs? Alcohol? Pornography? Mental illness? Or maybe narcissism? Did you pick up any of these? If so, I have a plan to help you change those habits! When you are damaged, there are two pathways to take:

#1. Share the pain: when you became a teen or adult, did you do the same thing to another kid? Did you pass that behavior and hurt on? Did you rob life from someone else?

#2. Heal and move forward, or just try to bury it and move forward.

When I was eight to nine years old, I found a male family member, who was a teenager, trying to molest another male family member who was only six or seven years old. It was completely by accident that I stumbled upon it. Luckily, I began yelling, and penetration did not occur. I ran and told the adults; they all looked at me like I spoke Greek! I yelled it out like four times!

Again, no one said anything! I saw no disciplinary action, nor did I hear about any later. I have no clue if any offenses had ever happened to the teenage family member that caused him to want to pass it on to another. I wondered if anyone was listening to him. What happened? Was it another family secret? One thing is for sure., I don't think anyone was getting help!

So, which path did you take? If your time of choosing hasn't come up yet, start thinking now! What choice do you think is the best choice to make? What do you want to share with another person? The hurt? Or the healing process? Do you want to be a person who has the answers to the problem? Or do you want to be the person who causes the problem?

I can tell you from experience that God has a plan for you! His love is all about taking what was meant for evil against you and turning it into something that will benefit you (Genesis 50:20), just as I am writing this book now to you. Yes, it hurts that the start in life they gave me was not up to par with their capabilities! Yes, it hurts that people could take advantage of me because of it. Yes, it hurts that money and material things precede me and my sister. But it no longer matters when your focus becomes your God-given destiny and calling! It no longer matters if your parents are remorseful or not about the neglect, abuse, etc., they put you through!

You must also understand that they grew up with hurt, a lack of love, and their problems both with grandparents and caregivers. They only gave what they had to give! Can we really blame them? It's all about knowledge and personal choices! After a while, you get tired of crying and hurting… and even thinking about it. Hosea 4:6 says my people perish for lack of knowledge!

I had no plans to write a book for teenagers. However, this book is also for adults and serves as closure for me. I don't have to carry it anymore or think about it alone! I am choosing to help solve the problem instead of passing it along! I chose to break the cycle by giving my children all the things that were missing in my life! Lol.

Reading the bible and getting to know God has relieved me from much pain. I look back now and see how I came from parents who taught me very little. See me now so confident, content, and full of knowledge and wisdom! Well, that was due to God alone, sending me the right resources, people, and much more.

My parents could never have done that! They were not equipped to do so. Your caregivers are the same – not equipped to do so. God should be your source. You can wait for a staff member, teacher, or whoever to help you, but you may be waiting and wishing for a while.

I no longer expect my parents/caregivers to support me in any way, nor do I sit and wait for remorsefulness. I focus on the one who filled my mind with knowledge and wisdom and revealed my gifts, talents, and values! I keep my eye on the one person – God – who directs my everyday steps on how to use my singing, what door to walk through to increase my finances, what dance performance people will support and enjoy, and best of all, what books to write and why!!!

My purpose in life is to help heal others, whether through a song – I sing with a sultry voice – that touches people every time I open my mouth… or dance. I dance to bring joy and excitement to others… or a speech. I speak to open minds and hearts alike. I give LOVE!!! How does a kid who grew up without love become a beacon of love? How do I know this to be true, you ask?

Example 1: I met a friend of a friend I did not know at a club one night. I hugged her at the end of the night before getting into my car. When I hugged her, she began to cry. I didn't understand why, so I asked if she was okay. She said, "Yes." I later found out why she was crying. She said, "I don't know… but when I hugged you, I felt warm. It was like love all over me." I also later found out that she was in an abusive relationship and did not know Jesus.

Example 2: When I meet men who like me, they all say the same thing: "You give me life" or "We don't have to be in a relationship. I just want to be a part of your life." The last guy in 2021 told me, "You just don't know how depressed I've been; you bring life to me."

God gave me love to give to others without me knowing it. He took what was meant as bad and made me become what I was missing (love); he turned it into good for others! Your trauma isn't for you!!! It is for others! I did not have sex with any of these men, and some still stay in touch via text message, maybe once or twice a year. They follow me on FB or IG.

Example 3: Every little kid I babysit, whether for a stranger or family, asks me the same question!!!! "Do you love me?" How crazy is that?!!! I gently look at them and say, yes! Why? Because I understand the importance of answering a child's question directly and sincerely. It is a life changer!

Even my special needs clients ask me the same thing, "Shema, you love me? It's unmistakably crazy! In return for my effortless, God-given love, these people give me so much love back, and I didn't really do anything but be me! Let the church say yes and Amen! I hear you, Lord! Lol

God will speak and guide you the same way if you open your heart and trust him! (Psalm 119:105). Don't expect family or friends to understand your purpose... they don't know your full story, they don't know your prayers, they don't know your purpose or God's plan for your life! They may not even know God. A relationship with God is very personal and tailor-made just for you. Others cannot advise you on which path to take on your journey to a new, redefined life. They may not know all your gifts and talents. You may not know them yet, but how can they tell you?

I would like to extend an offer to you. If you are reading this – hurt and crying – and unsure how to begin this process, let me tell you. You didn't have the mom or dad you should have had; no one cared, no one stood up to protect you, and no one loved you. You were neglected and/or abused.

Today, I am your mom! I'm sorry. I apologize for not loving you. I apologize for not protecting you. I am so sorry for abusing you. I am so sorry for neglecting you. I'm sorry for choosing everything else over you. I apologize for using and exploiting you. I regret the hurtful things I said to you and about you. I'm so sorry that I did not support and guide you in a positive, nurturing way. I love you so much, and I hope you will forgive me.

God will restore you! My restoration resulted in putting myself in dancing and singing classes, modeling and acting classes, coaching sessions, therapy, and college! I didn't think I was smart enough to go to college! I have written and produced songs and music videos.

I've ripped the runway, acted on TV shows, been in commercials, and performed on live shows! I did all this with three kids as a single mother!!! By the grace of God! I didn't see any of it coming; I only saw pieces. Do not look at your darkness and misery as "that's the end." There is more! Joy comes in the morning! (Psalm 30:5)

So again, I ask you, which path will you take? #1 or #2? Will you choose to hold on to bitterness, hatred, sorrow, and unforgiveness? Or will you choose the difficult road to freedom, healing, happiness, forgiveness, joy, and success?

I pray you chose #2, heal, and move forward!

Holding on to bitterness, hurt, unforgiveness, and hatred can lead to physical illnesses, faster aging of the skin, and advanced mental age, not to mention a shorter life! (Deuteronomy 5:33) Make no mistake. Just because you forgive someone does NOT mean you have to forget or maintain a relationship with them! Some people will try to tell you this. It is not so! Follow God's direction. Complete the worksheet at the end of this page, and let's see where you land! (Psalm 40:2).

Listen to the track: Praise is Due (album I Am)

Chapter 9
Worksheet

Before starting these worksheets, it is required that you write every answer down! Do Not think of the answers only! Please write below each question!

1. Have you forgiven your offender(s)?

2. Are you ready to forgive? If not, begin to pray and prepare yourself to forgive. This will be a lifelong practice! You might as well start now!

3. Have you forgiven yourself? Yes or no?
This is even harder than forgiving your offender.

4. Write down below what things you need to forgive yourself for. Read them daily and say: I forgive myself for_____, _____,_____. Repeat this as needed for everything you listed.
Ex: I had to forgive myself for choosing the wrong person to marry because it cost me more than I was willing to pay! I couldn't fully blame him. The choice was mine; no one forced me to marry him.

5. What do you choose to pass on to another? Hurt and offenses? Or help and healing?

6. What do you stand for?
Ex: I stand for love, healing, righteousness, protection of the innocent, forward movement.

7. What expectations do you need to let go of?
Ex: Expecting your caregivers to change, an apology, validation from others?

8. Who should know you better than anyone?
Answer: "me"

9. What is the #1 thing you must do in this life?
Answer: Find my identity!

10. What future endeavors await you that you cannot see?

11. What are your dreams?

Listen to my track, In His Presence Part 1!

Chapter 10
Relationships and Mistakes

The #1 thing I have learned throughout my life is to take the good with the bad, the bitter with the sweet, and look for the silver lining in all the darkness! It sounds good when you say it, huh? Lol. It sounded good when I wrote it, too!

It's painful and can be scary. After all, there is no rule book or strategy for calculating your bitterness. Yet, we must have relationships and trust each other, at least to a certain extent. Plus, we all make mistakes, and it's not wholly avoidable. Your bitterness could be something that seems so simple to someone else but is traumatic to you

What will be the mistake someone makes against you? How do you tell? Will they cheat? Lie? Betray you? Steal from you? Sabotage you? Kill you? Perhaps they will be perfect! What kind of lie or betrayal do you think you could get past? Which kind could you NOT get past?

Everyone has boundaries, whether they know it or not! For those who do not know, they usually end up hurting or killing someone. Someone says #snapped#. For me, I could never get past a person molesting or harming my children. When I look at guys to date, I am super focused on signs or possibilities that he may be "suspect." I can never marry or "be with" a guy who likes to abuse kids, including mentally!

When you have been abused/neglected, it is very easy to attract people who are familiar with where you come from. You may even start by building relationships that are comfortable for you. (Not always a positive thing). I implore you, dear reader, whoever you are, do not become your trauma and make odd, perverted relationships with others, kids, or the vulnerable. When you do the opposite, you become a symbol of change, strength, endurance, and hope! I hope that others like you can also change! Bring healing and wholeness to this world by nurturing our young, not "eating them up" like they are a delicacy!

Picture 1997 West Las Vegas, Nevada, in the "Big Carrie Arms" neighborhood. A deacon of one of the local churches is shacking up with a lady and her two daughters, ages two and four. These were my neighbors. She told me he was abusive, so I asked her several times why she stayed with him. She replied, "I don't know." One day, I saw him come home early and walk across the way to the babysitter's house. Five minutes later, I see him holding the four-year-old's hand and walking her to the house. My first thought was, "Where is the other little girl?" My second thought was, "he's molesting that girl."

I couldn't prove it, though. Two days later, the babysitter walks over to my house and tells me, "I kept the girls last night, and one of them woke up crying. When I asked her, Baby, what's wrong?" she said, "My butt hurts." Then, I asked her, "Baby, why does your butt hurt?" She said, "He always pushes it on me and makes me suck on it." My third thought was, "I knew it!"

He was taken to jail, but someone bailed him out. He was ordered to stay away from their house. Unfortunately, he came back, and they moved. I told her many things and gave her resources to get help; we also discussed protecting her girls!!!! I pray that she did. I chose to play my part in such a short relationship and did not stay silent.

Relationships matter, even if you have a friendship or are in a relationship with someone you KNOW is a rapist, child molester, abuser, narcissist, or trafficker. Maybe YOU are the abuser. Don't sit silent! Don't be still! Don't procrastinate! Get help! There is nothing wrong with admitting your dirty secrets to a trained professional therapist or joining a support group for people who have the same issues. If you take those steps, it would be a step toward saving lives (yours, theirs, and those watching you!) – a body, a soul, a spirit, a family!

Complete the worksheets at the end of this chapter. It will take you through how to begin to break free from your addiction, abuse, neglect, and exploitation of the vulnerable. As well as how to find forgiveness.

Here is a crazy story for you! Can you imagine ME being a phone sex girl? Well, I was! Lol. I learned a lot! One day, I received a call from a young man who seemed to lie about his age so he could make the call! As we got into our chat, he began to tell me how his sister's last class in school gym class was and how she sweats a lot. He said he likes to wait until she takes her shower; then he goes into the restroom and sniffs her underwear! Someone says, GROSS! I figured he would eventually end up raping his sister. Hopefully, he did not! I quit the job after a month as the conversations were crazy. I thought, wow! This is what children have to live with? Some guys were okay, and some were perverted.

Another choice I made was to be the opposite of my trauma: to offer safe and trustworthy babysitting services on Craigslist (CL)! I do this to catch kids who may fall through the cracks. Anyone looking to babysit on CL doesn't have the funds to afford proper care, which leaves kids open to "things" happening. So, I charge the price below to beat out the predators AND protect the kids. But again, these creeps have always seemed to be in my world one way or another!

Creep #1 calls my phone, and as I'm talking about my babysitting services, he is on the phone "jacking off!" (masturbating).
Creep #2 emails me asking, "Do you have a male who can do anything they want to my kids?" After I explained to him that I don›t engage in those kinds of perverse activities and he shouldn't either, he explained, "It's not hurting them; it feels good, and that's how my parents raised me..." Long story short, I contacted Craigslist to see what they were doing to contain or discourage predators from using their platform to groom and molest kids. I haven't heard anything back yet!

It's been five months. I also sent a request to the local news station to investigate it. I haven't heard anything back yet! What kind of relationships will you build (hurt vs. healed), and what will you stand for? What do you choose to STOP tolerating?

It sounds easier said than done, but remember you are not alone! Take one step, and God will take two! All you must do is make the choice! Yes, I will get help, I will try, and yes, I will go through the process to be a role model for those coming behind me!!

There is one relationship you can never make a mistake with! Your relationship with Jesus! Many think you must get together before you can talk to him, think about him, or even go to a church. That is NOT true. That completely defeats the purpose of his death. It's when you really mess up and know that you have no control to stop or change it! When you get to that point, you pray and go before your creator and cry for help! (2 Cor. 12:9-11). That is the point where he will meet you: when you are broken!!!!!!!!!! When you are truly, utterly broken!!!!!!!! That's where he finds true remorse from you, where, hopefully, he will find true repentance (turning away from your perpetual act of sin). There is hope for you if you really want it!

For those who have no repentance or remorse, I have a message for you (male or female): the Lord God, our creator, has heard the cries of his most treasured, and the tears have added up. Your heart is hardened, and if you do not acknowledge your wrongdoings and confess them to the proper authority (pastor, hotline, google, local resources, etc.), your days are numbered!

Turn from your ways and ask the Lord to soften your heart and help you accomplish this difficult task. (Matthew 18:6). This is your final warning, and vengeance will be mine, says the Lord! (This applies whether you are a believer in God or not!) So, repent! (Google it.)

Resources:

- https://sex-addictionrecovery.com/legal-system-treatment/?gclid=CjwKCAw682TBhATEiwA9crl3zi3OfDAD-yLuwaD8kU83Ud_PjiEA4YNpMYR_ysL_qfp86EX4wje5xoC504QAvD_BwE

- Phone: 855-422-1912

- Sexoffenderonestopresources.com

- National Domestic Violence hotline.
  Phone: 800-799-7233

- https://www.samhsa.gov/find-help/national-helpline (addictions)

Those are just a few resources to help you get started! Good luck! You are truly sincere in my prayers, as are those of others who have read this book! We all have issues (sins) ranging from fornication, adultery, homosexuality, bearing false witness (lying), dishonoring our parents, using God's name in vain (God damn), murder, stealing, idolatry (worshipping money or other people, statues, animals, thereby putting other things in a higher priority above God), pride, gluttony, arrogance.

I get it. God has made a way to be forgiven, saved, and changed with a better life!
It boils down to a choice! What will your choice be? Will you choose to have a relationship with him or try to do it yourself and carry your baggage throughout life?

I know a few people who are alcoholics. They always tell me, "I can do this myself. I don't need AA groups. I watch them year after year continue to drink even though they confess that they have a problem. I think it's better to give a year of my life getting help to become a new person than to be addicted year after year with no progress!

Jesus loves even the offender. Through his love, he has offered you an opportunity for redemption. He forces himself on no one, but he WILL turn his back and walk away from you if you choose not to receive him and say no to him. (Matthew 10:14)

As a Licensed Vocational Nurse, I have seen many things! While working in a hospital in East Texas, I had a patient come in: a slender white male in his mid-twenties or early thirties. I knew from the moment I saw his countenance that something was terribly wrong! He sat in a wheelchair, slumped over, with his head hanging low. He was wearing inmate clothes from one of the local penitentiaries. This grey gloom sat over him like a cloud. It looked like his soul had been snatched out of him.

Another nurse came over and told me he had been brought over from one of the prison units. As I watched the guard roll him into the exam room, I had a thought: "He has been gang raped, but I could be wrong." As the other nurse was still talking, I heard her say, "They got him in a room and five guys raped him." Now, how did I know that? Even adults go through trauma. The doctor stitched him up, and it was a wrap!

I also worked as a substitute teacher for a while. One day, I took a break to use the restroom and noticed feces on the wall and all over one of the stalls! This is a classic sign that a child has been molested. I notified the principal, so hopefully, we could locate the child and get them some help. Unfortunately, most kids won't say anything. Usually, it is because they are afraid, embarrassed, ashamed, or they don't know how to say something. They have often been manipulated to think that nothing is wrong with it. It's a good thing, or they are made to feel like no one will care.

I encourage everyone reading this book, whether you have suffered a trauma or not, to KEEP YOUR EYES, EARS, AND HEART OPEN! BE AWARE! The vulnerable need our help! Again, as a nurse, I have even seen mentally and physically disabled people abused, neglected, and exploited. They may not say one word. Be an advocate for someone. Lend an open ear and ask questions. Above all, make sure the help you get for them will not destroy the opportunity or worsen things.

I watched a woman on TV giving her testimony in Dallas, Texas. Her mother had sold her to a man at fourteen years old. This was aired in January of 2022. For over twenty years, this man had abused her. She finally got the nerve to tell someone at her church (the only place he would let her go). The pastor's wife didn't believe her and told her to keep it quiet (old slavery mindset). Then the pastor's wife told her husband! The man beat her unconscious. The neighbor saw and heard what was going on through their bathroom window. She ran home, got her gun, and then started shooting inside their house at the husband! She saved her neighbor's life!!!!!

You must know who is equipped and qualified to handle abused and neglected people correctly! It can cost someone their life!

I pray as you read this: Lord, let both offender and victims alike feel, experience, and know your love! Anoint and use those reading this book and whose hearts you are touching right now. Lord, bring healing, wholeness, restoration, courage, knowledge, and wisdom to every person who reads this in Jesus' name so that they may intervene and help save a soul, a life, or a spirit from being destroyed or perverted.

I declare that each person who takes action with these instruments will receive a quick experience in you with all their relationships! Heavenly Father, give them an encounter with you that will change their world! All because their response to you was, "YES, I receive you!" All because they touched what was dear to your heart (the little ones)! I pray grace for those who have decided to work on their repentance for abusing the vulnerable.

I declare a supernatural encounter with the Holy Spirit that will sustain them in walking in victory and overcoming their habitual sins against you! In the precious blood of the sacrificial lamb (Jesus), amen!!!

Listen to tracks A Prayer and A Message (album I Am)

Chapter 10
Worksheet

Before starting these worksheets, it is required that you write every answer down! Do not think of the answers only! Please write below each question!

1. Are you staying silent about things you know are not right?

2. Do you have an addiction that you need help with?

Are you being honest? Yes or no?

The FIRST step is to see that you have a problem (sex, drugs, alcohol, gambling, etc.).

3. Which one listed above do you need to do multiple times per day? (This indicates that you may have an addiction or a problem.)

4. Do you need to lie, cover up, or avoid talking about your habit with others? Yes or no? (If yes, this is a clear sign that you have an addiction.)

Now, what do you do? Locate someone you trust, not a "yes man"!

Call a national or local hotline; you can begin anonymously. This is the healthiest thing you can do for yourself and others! You can also "web search" for sex offender therapy/counseling (if sex is your issue).

Sometimes, when you have done unthinkable or even horrific acts, it's hard to believe that God can forgive you or love you. It's hard to imagine that he could even change you into a new person, but he can!!

Continue to read through this book. Pray the prayers of repentance and salvation. Follow the steps and look for change! God still loves you! He just hates your actions. He will forgive you if it's truly from your heart and you take the steps needed to be a healer of pain, not a giver of pain.

5. Are you ready and willing to change?

If not, pray and ask God to get you ready! Call and get help, anyway, and see what happens!

Chapter 11
Are Parents Good or Bad?

I don't want to give anyone the impression that my parents were horrible! Remember the good with the bad, the bitter with the sweet? Yep, they come together! They come in three: the good, the bad, and the ugly! In the mid-2000s, there was this saying kids would utter to each other, sometimes as a joke: "Oooh, you are ugly, you lookin' like yo daddy, boy/girl you ugly!"

Actually, my parents are the coolest, most fashionable people you'd want to know! (This includes my stepparents) I would describe my father as cool, calm, collected, fun, outgoing, energetic, 100% hustler, creative, strong, intelligent, a do-it-all handyman, diverse, a leader, inspiring, and a trendsetter!

My mother was a model once upon a time! She has fashion and beauty on lock, hands down! I would describe her as kind, gentle, understanding, the strongest woman I know, adventurous, spontaneous, forgiving, patient, stylish, funny, spicey, spunky, creative, and crazy! Lol.

They both gave me a love for music, arts, travel, dance, fashion, style, creativity, and soul! When my parents had a "good" day, they would dance together. Music was played in the house every weekend! My father liked to paint portraits and participate in outdoor sports! Mom spent most of her time trying to recuperate her body and get her mind right. The tough skin I developed through my old friend's "neglect" was called endurance, mixed with survival skills and courage... or you can just say "ESSC"   . Under all the dysfunction was a silver lining!

Imagine getting stepparents! I spoke to a young friend of mine, whose name is Shun. I sat and listened as she explained how she did not want stepparents and how inconvenient they would be! Lol. So, I shared my experience with her! Granted, my stepfather is my former best friend's dad! Or should I say my now stepsister's dad? Do you want to know something even crazier? How crazy is it that my stepfather will help me quicker and easier than my father?

How crazy is it that my stepmother would tell me things like, "You are a wonderful daughter. I love you."? My mother has never told me that before! I didn't know mothers said things like that. At first, I thought she was joking, but then I thought maybe she meant it. It felt strange but good! On top of that, she was a singer   ! I would listen to her rehearse before a show: she would sing around Las Vegas. That was so amazing to me, and I felt connected to her just because of that one simple thing. And there was her cooking, of course   !

She had an amazing opportunity to become a backup singer for the great Gregory Hines, an amazing African American singer, actor, and tap dancer! I liked this lady, and I saw a lot of silver linings!

God can get things you need in your life, although they may not come in the way you first thought or from whom! My stepmother brought a voice into my life with consistent food, open ears, patience, grace, kindness, creativity, and fashion. She was an example of friendships between women as I watched her with her friends. She exemplified strength, trust, honesty, class, loyalty, and forgiveness. She was all those things and more! Funny, she seemed to be the only sane one out of all my parents!

My stepfather, many, many years later, changed his ugly ways of bringing lies and broken relationships into my life. He added laughter, humor, support, open ears, good restaurants, entertainment, and empathy. This man is hilarious!! I can only say the nice part (the sweets) of these stories because I have had time to heal, forgive, and find my identity.

As you go through your process, one day, you will also be able to talk about your past positively, as long as you let go of the bitterness and move forward. It will be hard, but it is doable! The sweets will come around again!!

This is my testament: sometimes, the offender can make positive changes! I haven't seen or heard of my sister throwing any more shoes, either! So,   , it's possible! What you need will often come through someone other than your family or caregivers.

Example: Imagine a twenty-four-year-old young lady with a fresh, new baby. One week later, she begins to hemorrhage and ends up in the emergency room at the hospital. They are unable to stop the bleeding. As she lies in bed, losing control of all of her bodily functions, she gathers just enough strength to ask the nurse, "Can I make a phone call, please?" The nurse says, "Sure, hon, you want to call your mom, huh?" The young lady looks confused and can't understand why the nurse would say something like that.

The young lady looked at her and replied, "No, I'm calling my kids' babysitter." The nurse looked at the young lady with surprise. Kids? When the young lady first went into the hospital, it was 11:00 pm on a Monday. When I came through after surgery, it was 2:00 pm Wednesday! No one was there when I opened my eyes. I stayed in the hospital one more day, and then I had to get a ride home.

As I pondered whom to call, I began to dial numbers on my phone. I called the assistant pastor of my church and his wife; they came to the hospital. Once they arrived, we spoke for a while; then the pastor's wife, Rachel, asked me, "Shema, why didn't you call your parents?" I sat silent for a moment because that question was again asked about my parents, and I didn't know the answer immediately. I began to think. 1. They must keep bringing up my parents for a reason. 2. Why didn't I think about calling my parents? They literally never came to my mind! I just knew I could call the church. So, I told her, as my eyes teared up, "I'm sorry, but I didn't know who else to call."

As you read this chapter, notice all the sweet and silver linings I point out. My pastor and second lady came to check on me as soon as I called! God told me, "Shema, I will come for you when no one else comes. When no one else loves you, I will love you." These are some ways that God says, "I love you!"

Example: God's love in my life: every time I DIDN'T get molested or picked up to be in R. Kelly's haram, lol. Every time, he kept me from being killed (when I got jumped or when someone was about to literally stab me in my back). He protected me when I was in the middle of a shootout. He sent someone who would pay my power bill when my well-to-do parents wouldn't help or when he ensured that I had one aunt willing to walk it out… and not just talk it out! There were the cousins who girded under me and gave me input and support while I was in the streets with no good sense!

His love was protecting me when I was rolling with one of the craziest OGs in Las Vegas and when I had kids with one of Vegas's biggest ballers! All of these are ways that God gives his love to you! He sends it through people, but mostly angels!

Was I wrong when I felt that I should be able to call my parents for any reason? You should be able to depend on and believe that your parents/caregivers love you enough that they will stop everything to help you! This is a correct belief and how it should be!!! It's up until a certain age – at least in the early twenties. For my children and me, was it their mid-late twenties? – decisions are still sketchy! However, we do not all get that, i.e., everyone WON'T get that. So, now what?

I heard Bishop T.D. Jakes says that people won't spend ten minutes to help you if you need a bill paid or a ride, but they will spend two to three hours at your funeral! Cold, isn't it

Dear reader, are you able to receive his love? Love that's NOT like what people give? Everyone says they want love, but most people do not know what love is! My sister and I sat at the bar one day with Dad, and we asked, "Daddy, what is love?" He heaved a sigh, began to describe love, then hesitated. At this point, I'm around twenty-seven and still trying to figure out what love is. Lmbo! We did not get a clear answer!

The biblical definition of love is 1 Corinthians 13:4–8a (ESV). Love is patient and kind; love does not envy or boast. It is not arrogant or rude. It does not insist in its way; it is not irritable or resentful; it does not rejoice at wrongdoing but rejoices in the truth. There are so many things he protects us from that we don't even see! That is love!

Sacrificing for others, that is love! Life isn't perfect. We must take the good with the bad.

What are the silver linings or the "sweets" in your situation? What silver linings did your caregivers/parents share with you through their talents, character, or hobbies? How did those things influence you? Your life?

Complete the worksheets at the end of this chapter! They will help you to see your circumstances through different lenses. Hopefully, they will help you forgive and shift your mind and emotions towards a love that's better than our faulted and failed human love.

Are parents good or bad? Both exist and have some good, bad, and ugly! No one is perfect! Some parents discipline appropriately, some parents don't discipline at all, and some take discipline too far – i.e., they are abusive!

Some parents/caregivers are passive, while some are aggressive. Some are just weird, some are controlling, some are introverts, some are psychotic, some are mentally disabled, some are Ill, some are loving, and some are compassionate, nurturing, sincere, honest, dedicated, active parents. Unfortunately, we don't get to choose what we get!

The statistics of child maltreatment and neglect show the severity of the problem!!! 3.9 million child maltreatment referral reports were received in 2020. Child abuse reports involved 7.1 million children. 90.6% of victims are maltreated by one or both parents. Only 3.1 million children received prevention and post-response services. 124,360 children received foster care services. 470,297 victims (74.9%) are neglected. 101,961 victims (17.5%) are physically abused. 57,963 victims (9.3%) were sexually abused. 39,652 victims (6.1%) are psychologically maltreated.

The highest rate of child abuse is in children under age one (25.1 per 1,000). Annual estimate: 1,750 children died from abuse and neglect in 2020. Five children die every day from child abuse. Sixty-eight (67.8%)

percent of all child fatalities were younger than three years old. 80.6% of child fatalities involve at least one parent.

Of the children who died, 73.7% suffered child neglect. Of the children who died, 42.6% suffered physical abuse either exclusively or in combination with another maltreatment type. 46.4% of children who die from child abuse are under one year.

Boys had a higher child fatality rate than girls (2.99 boys and 2.05 girls per 100,000). Almost 58,000 children are sexually abused. For 2020, 35 states report 953 unique victims of sex trafficking. For victims of the sex trafficking maltreatment type, the majority (88.6%) are female, and 10.9 percent are male.

It is estimated that between 50-60% of maltreatment fatalities are not recorded on death certificates. Child abuse crosses all socioeconomic and educational levels, religions, and ethnic and cultural groups 14% of all men in prison and 36% of women in prison in the USA were abused as children, about twice the frequency as in the general population. Children who experience child abuse and neglect are approximately nine times more likely to become involved in criminal activity. (Source: AmericanSPCC.org)

Notice that they do not include spiritual abuse in the statistics. Yet every CPS/APS office in this huge country in the USA is well aware of it! They do not say anything about it and do not want to touch on spiritual conversations. Yet, at the same time, they need to have protocols and plans for it! If I encounter it, I know that they also do!!!

You can bet that one out of every three children in your classroom, your dance class, your neighborhood, your sports team, and your family is being maltreated in some way. Please be aware of it and be a source of help and support!

Sometimes, strange things happen to me. This is one sign of knowing that God is real! Strangely enough, In 2021, whenever I was in Las Vegas and took an Uber, the driver would look at me and say, "I used to be a witch, and Jesus saved me." Or "I was into witchcraft and demons, but now I am a Christian." This happened to me three or four times! I sat there and thought, why are they telling me this? Do they say this to everyone who gets in their car?

I normally like to sit silent. I just want to get home after work! Finally, I began to say, "Praise God and welcome to the Kingdom." Some would tell me about their struggles with how the devil was trying to hold onto them, how difficult it was to find a new group of friends, etc. They were very interesting stories!

If you choose a relationship with Christ, you have a Father who will protect you, even in dire situations. His presence is a repellent against evil! If His Spirit lives IN you, no other spirit can rule or dominate you!!! That's guaranteed by His blood!!

As a licensed nurse and business owner, I have had the opportunity to work with special needs (mental and physical disabilities) populations. In 2016, I received a referral for a new client named Brian. At first meeting this client, he was so afraid that he yelled and jumped up and down. He was frantic! This young man was only eleven years old at that time. I recommended to the parents that we try again next week. Mom explained that she was removing him from another facility because her son refused to go.

When he returned the next week, he was calm enough to stay. I noticed he would not sit and acted as if he was in pain. Even in the car, he would lean to his side but would not sit flat on his buttocks. I called the referring company that had sent Brian to me and called the parents. I asked them both if he had any history of molestation. The referring company said, "Not that we know of." The parent said, "No".

I noticed that he also manifested behaviors that revealed his trust had been broken. After two weeks of partaking in my services, he relaxed and began to sit normally. He seemed to have trust in me now. Months later, the mom revealed that her son did have some strange habits once upon a time. He would come home and try to stick objects into his butt, and he attempted to burn the house down!

She also reported that the previous facility he was going to went out of business, and they couldn't contact anyone from there anymore. I was convinced that her son had been molested at the last facility; that's why he refused to go back! He could not speak verbally, but he was definitely trying to say something! I explained the signs of abuse to his mom. I tried to comfort her as her head hung low in guilt, shame, hurt, and betrayal at what someone had done to her son.

In 2022, I received another nonverbal client, Shelly. Unfortunately, she had signs that she, too, had had sexual encounters. When I brought it up, the family member wrote it off as something else, even though Shelly, too, was removed from her last foster care provider. I will probably run into these situations for the rest of my life!

Many family members (caretakers) mean well, but they are not aware or may refuse to believe that someone would do such a thing to a kid, let alone a disabled person! I have received phone calls about little brothers (13-14) molesting infants and toddlers, moms finding blood in their baby's diapers, and more.

I was sitting at home watching the news in 2021. A story was being told about a nursing home where a nonverbal, non-ambulatory, crippled woman gave birth to a baby in her bed. No one ever knew she was pregnant until the baby came! How did that happen? Well, one of the male CNAs had been raping her. They were able to identify who did it because the victim was white, and the baby came out black. Only one black man was working in that unit! Wow, she couldn't speak, but she made a statement!

Again, I encourage you to be aware and knowledgeable about signs, including silence and demeanor. Forgive your offenders and pick up God's plan for your life! It is a lot easier!

Chapter 11
Worksheet

Before starting these worksheets, it is required that you write every answer down! Do Not think of the answers only! Please write below each question!

1. Can you list some of the good things about your caregiver(s)? If so, list them below!
Ex: fun, funny, cool, ambitious, creative. Etc.

2. Are you open to God using someone to help or bless you, someone you didn't expect?

3. If you had/have step-parents, can you write 1-5 things they did for you that your parents/caregivers wouldn't/didn't do?

A.
B.
C.
D.
E.

4. Are you able to speak about your past trauma AND experiences with some added sweetness? Yes or no?

If not, give it more time and continue to take steps towards healing, more knowledge, and forgiveness. Again, I tell you, "Look for the silver lining."

5. Who has God been sending to you that you may have taken for granted?

6. Do you sacrifice for others?

7. How do you express love to others?

To strangers?

8. Are your eyes open?

Are you making yourself available to those who are vulnerable and may need help? If not, here are some steps you can take now! Slow down and look at people patiently, look at body language and grooming habits, become an active listener, get involved with your local entities for public training offered, start neighborhood discussions on the topic, educate yourself, and above all, take action!

Appendix

Depression Symptoms in Children and Teens

Common signs and symptoms of depression in children and teenagers are similar to those in adults, but there can be some differences. In younger children, symptoms of depression may include sadness, irritability, clinginess, worry, aches and pains, refusing to go to school, or being underweight.

In teens, symptoms may include sadness, irritability, feeling negative and worthless, anger, poor performance or poor attendance at school, feeling misunderstood and extremely sensitive, using recreational drugs or alcohol, eating or sleeping too much, self-harm, loss of interest in normal activities, and avoidance of social interaction.

Depression symptoms in older adults: depression is not a normal part of growing older, and it should never be taken lightly. Unfortunately, depression often goes undiagnosed and untreated in older adults, and they may feel reluctant to seek help. Symptoms of depression may be different or less obvious in older adults, such as:

Memory difficulties or personality changes.

Physical aches or pain.

Fatigue, loss of appetite, sleep problems, or loss of interest in sex not caused by a medical condition or medication.

Often wanting to stay at home, rather than going out to socialize or doing new things.

Suicidal thinking or feelings, especially in older men.

When to see a doctor: If you feel depressed, make an appointment to see your doctor or mental health professional as soon as you can. If you're reluctant to seek treatment, talk to a friend or loved one, any health care professional, a faith leader, or someone you trust.

When to get emergency help:

If you think you may hurt yourself or attempt suicide, call 911 or your local emergency number immediately.

Consider these options if you're having suicidal thoughts:

Call your doctor or mental health professional.

Call a suicide hotline number: in the U.S., call the National Suicide Prevention Lifeline at 1-800-273-TALK (1-800-273-8255). Use that same number and press "1" to reach the Veterans Crisis Line.

Reach out to a close friend or loved one.

Contact a minister, spiritual leader, or someone in your faith community. If you have a loved one who is in danger of suicide or has made a suicide attempt, make sure someone stays with that person. Call 911 or your local emergency number immediately. If you think you can do so safely, take the person to the nearest hospital emergency room.

(Source: Mayoclinic.org)

About the Author

Shema Ladd has served the community for the last twenty-eight years in leadership roles such as the single women's ministry at her church, where she's counseled, served on praise teams, and sang in the choir. She has participated in prayer shut-ins and volunteered in conferences, serving as needed, all while raising her children. She participated in natural disaster relief efforts such as Hurricane Katrina and the COVID-19 pandemic.

Shema volunteered with housing refugees at church while supplying shelter, food, hygiene products, compassion, multiple resources, and counseling. In the Austin, Texas Statesman newspaper, she was recognized for her vaccination efforts to the disabled community as an essential worker (nurse) during the COVID outbreak.

She has spent time ministering the message of salvation in downtown Austin multiple times and praying for and feeding the homeless, prostitutes, and drug addicts while volunteering anywhere else as needed. She has also participated in community benefits like Cancer and Kidney Walks of America.

This fearless spirit-filled woman of God has served and studied under the five-fold ministry with leaders and instructors from around the world, including Germany, Mexico, Ghana, France, Texas, Romania, Hawaii, and multiple U.S. states, while focusing on systematic theology and knowing God's divine nature through relationships.

In 2011, Shema added a brief description of her life story and published it in a multi-story book, "The Journey Continues; More Stories from East Texas." A few years later, Shema was acknowledged in a second Book, "Loved as Promised" by J. Ladd Johnson.

This heavy-hitting pioneer is described as one of the most inspirational motivators and innovators in her community and her space. She is a four-time CEO business owner, starting in the Beauty industry as a nail technician, providing nail services and consulting – often counseling her clients. Shema began working in hotel spas on the Las Vegas Strip. After growing tired of working in a "right to hire/fire state," this amazing manicurist decided to make her way, starting "Nails by Shema." She developed her manicure, pedicure services, AND products representing her love of skincare! She innovated Margarita pedicures that made their way into international competitions. This creative go-getter became accustomed to winning first and third place for her acrylic work and nail art! Moving closer to her calling, Shema started her second business, Helping Communities Live.

As an LV Nurse Case Manager specializing in mental health for a nationwide billion-dollar company, Shema trained new employees and worked alongside psychologists, psychiatrists, social workers, therapists, physicians, families, and state governments! She is described by co-workers as "one of the best nurses around, fast on her feet and ready for a challenge."

Her business is centered on holistic care, mental health, behavior modifications, and life skills. She enjoys the psychology of it! Success has pushed her to a six-figure income and made her hungry for more!

Later, stepping into modeling, she did shoots for companies such as Nordstrom's, Alamo, Draft House, and Apple, Inc., which led her to start her third business, "Skills N Talents Modeling!" Since recently discovering her true God-given purpose, she decided to start her fourth business, Help Me Out! Life coaching is where she coaches people to discover their purpose by identifying their gifts and talents. She leads them to discover how to use their God-given talents to walk in purpose and have a transformational experience in life and abundance.

Her mission is for people to know who you are and whose you are and for them to serve their purpose on this earth—free from emotional, mental, and spiritual distress—while living an abundant, successful life filled with joy!

Follow Shema @ FB Shema Ladd, a personal development and premarital coach.

LinkedIn: Shema Ladd, personal development and premarital coach

YouTube: Shema Ladd, personal development and premarital coach

Acknowledgements

Special thanks to the ministries that have poured into my life and brought me to this point!

Childhood: Carver Baptist Church & Full Gospel deliverance church

Young adult: Mt. Zion Baptist Church with Pastor Wayne and Carla Arnold

Assistant pastors Wayne and Rachel Chaisson

Adult: Palestine Church (non-denominational) with

Pastors: Danny and Loretta Rodriguez, Apostle Dr. Ricky Paris, and wife Jane Paris.

Teachers Bill and Faye Byers, Evangelists Jeff and Milicent Collins, And Dr. Oliver and Monique Vanderpuye (whom I consider Dr. Oliver a prophet.)

And finally, Exchange Church (non-denominational) with pastors Tre and Carrie Rose.

Listen to the track "Shout Out" album.

Thank you for purchasing this book!

When I wrote this book (2022), my father was living, and the book's release was meant for 2023. Unfortunately, he passed since then (10/2023). I did not want to change any of the content, so I left it as is. Unfortunately, the passing of my father brought forth more betrayals and other family issues that I work through even today. The silver lining is this: I lived in the hospital with my father for eleven days before he passed. Because of my obedience to the Lord, he allowed me to go into spiritual places to witness the whole process! My father and I gained an understanding, and a lot of healing took place – mental, physical, and emotional. The Lord was very present and active in the entire situation . I had the privilege of helping my father transition spiritually and physically. The Lord opened a different spiritual realm to me during this time.

While I was enjoying the fruit of my obedience and watching how God deals with someone who has recently started doing the "work" needed to get into God's grace (my dad). I was being talked about, lied to, villainized, and some! Even though Dad and I were at complete peace, outsiders added drama and gossip to something peaceful and sweet. How does that happen? (Saved folks? Intelligent folks? Mostly religious, but mainly one who dabbled in witchcraft).

At the same time, those talking were missing God and what he was doing. As I sit, I start struck in awe of what I am witnessing between God and my father. God is tearing down the lies. He is fighting my battle in the earth realm while I am in the spirit realm

Oooh, to watch God work!

I was obedient in all aspects, regardless of outsiders and those who tried to block God's will out of ignorance. For this, a table was set before me in front of my enemies literally (See story in book # 2: coming soon!) As I stand in front of a crowd at a funeral, having the gift to see and hear in the spirit, I see people's sins, what they have done or said, and what God wants for them. I hear the Holy Spirit as he speaks. I see and hear those who are carrying demonic spirits.

It is a very difficult gift at times; it is bittersweet and not something you can always share with your family, especially if you are not preaching in a church and are known publicly for that gift. Just pray and understand you're calling. Accept God's will, timing, and your identity in the Kingdom of God!

These events have compelled me to write another book!

Keep your eyes open   . The next book will cover helping loved ones with spiritual transitioning, walking in the spirit, spiritual inheritances, witchcraft in the family, how to handle it, being born to parents with money, and how others and even stepparents may have an alternative motive in their views of you. God is in it all!

You will want to read this one; it is juicy! I may include gifts of the spirit and cover my match-making gift, highlighting the five couples I have connected through the obedience of Christ. Three are married to date, and two are engaged to get married in 2024 & 2025. I will be a bridesmaid in 2024! To God be the glory! Even without gratitude from some! (Bittersweet, silver linings.)

Keep me in your prayers as I write the next book and seek God for his will and guidance   God Bless.

> **Listen to the track: My Hamilton (album I Am)**

Try to rest in peace, Daddy; I know the Lord's servants are working with you to ensure you will be one of the first to rise. Continue to do the work, and I will see you soon   .

www.ingramcontent.com/pod-product-compliance
Lightning Source LLC
LaVergne TN
LVHW051038070526
838201LV00066B/4857